IMAGES
*of America*

# DEATH VALLEY

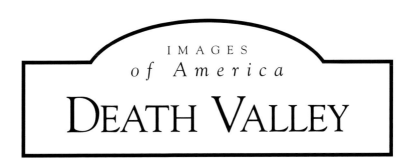

IMAGES
*of America*

# DEATH VALLEY

Robert P. Palazzo

ARCADIA
PUBLISHING

Published by Arcadia Publishing
Charleston, South Carolina

Printed in the United States of America

Library of Congress Catalog Card Number: 2007941842

For all general information contact Arcadia Publishing at:
Telephone 843-853-2070
Fax 843-853-0044
E-mail sales@arcadiapublishing.com
For customer service and orders:
Toll-Free 1-888-313-2665

Visit us on the Internet at www.arcadiapublishing.com

*To Vivianne, who has cheerfully endured both Death Valley the place
and Death Valley the book.*

# CONTENTS

# ACKNOWLEDGMENTS

I would like to thank the following individuals who provided either encouragement, help, or both during the course of this project: Dale Alberstone; David Grossberg; Jim Lorenzo; Michael Hecht; Reginald and Yvonne Hill; the late Tom G. Murray; Donald J. Palazzo, esq.; Blair Davenport, curator of Death Valley National Park Museum; Christine Giles, curator of Palm Springs Art Museum; Dean Bray; Daisy; and of course my wife, Vivianne, who offered many valuable suggestions and insights in addition to support. I also want to thank "T" and "J," who wish to remain anonymous, but they know who they are. In addition, my editor John Poultney has provided advice and help. I especially would like to thank Robert Varlotta, who encouraged and helped not only with this book but to whom I am indebted for my initial appreciation and understanding of the Death Valley area.

Photographs marked "Willard" are courtesy of Palm Springs Art Museum, Stephen H. Willard Photography Collection and Archive. Photographs marked "NPS photograph" are courtesy of National Park Service, Death Valley National Park. All photographs are courtesy of the Robert P. Palazzo Collection unless noted otherwise.

# INTRODUCTION

The Death Valley region is considered to include not only Death Valley itself—which is technically actually a basin and not a valley—but also the surrounding area that now encompasses the Death Valley National Park. The park itself was created in 1994 when the Desert Protection Act was signed into law, which added an additional 1.3 million acres to the 2 million that were already included when Death Valley was made a national monument in 1933. The park now contains 3.3 million acres, or approximately 3,000 square miles; is the largest park in size in the contiguous United States; and is visited by one million tourists each year. As vast as the area is, its permanent population is very small. Death Valley has always been considered a land of extremes. When the conditions are right, both the highest point in the contiguous United States (Mount Whitney) and the lowest (Badwater) can be seen from Dante's View. The bleak and inhospitable landscape has been given descriptive geographic names, beginning of course with the name Death Valley itself, and including Badwater, Breakneck Canyon, Burnt Wagons, Chaos Ridge, Coffin Canyon, Dead Man Pass, Devil's Cornfield, Dripping Blood Cliffs, Funeral Mountains, Furnace Creek, Hell Gate, Poison Spring, Starvation Canyon, and Suicide Pass. Yet Death Valley supports life: 91 species of mammals live in the area, as well as reptiles and amphibians, 346 species of birds, over 1,000 species of plants, and even 5 species of fish!

As with many other areas of the West, the history of Death Valley begins with its discovery and first visit by the "white man" in 1849. What makes Death Valley unique is that its discovery was also made by white women. Of course neither white men nor white women discovered Death Valley. Death Valley had been populated by the ancestors of the Timbisha Shoshone tribe for at least 1,000 years before 1849 and by others for many thousands of years before them. The Timbisha were a nomadic people with no written language, living in a remote and isolated land. This helps explain the lack of knowledge of the Death Valley region and its history among nonnative people. That all changed in 1849. A party of gold-seeking Easterners heading west to the California goldfields decided to split off from the main wagon train to take a shortcut they were told about in Salt Lake City, a route which led them through Death Valley. The shortcut proved illusory and they suffered immensely, enduring undue hardships with some loss of life. William Manly memorialized this story in his book *Death Valley in '49*, which captured the public's imagination.

Mining has been a part of Death Valley's story from the beginning. A member of the original party of 1849 found a rock of nearly pure silver, which he took with him to Mariposa and had made into a gunsight. Parties seeking to find the Lost Gunsight Mine have crossed Death Valley ever since. The first attempts were led by the Darwin French expeditions of 1850 and 1860 and met with little success. Darwin Falls in the national park and the town of Darwin just outside are named for Darwin French.

Spanish mining took place just west of Death Valley at Coso during the 1860s and provided an impetus to explore the area further. A number of government expeditions and surveys followed. In 1861, the U.S. and California Boundary Commission went through Death Valley, followed in 1866 by a survey party led by Nevada governor Henry Blasdell. The next year, the first military expedition was led by Lt. Charles Bendire, who scouted the Death Valley area looking for a route from the Owens Valley and Silver Peak to Pahranagat east of Death Valley in Nevada. The first of four Wheeler Survey Expeditions began in 1871 and the U.S. Department of Agriculture's Death Valley Expedition in 1891 resulted in the publication of several scientific books.

Although there was significant mining in the Panamints during the early 1860s that led to the creation of the Telescope Peak Mining District and the discovery of the Christmas Gift Mine, a significant mining discovery was made in December 1872 that led to the formation of the boom town of Panamint, located in Surprise Canyon. By the fall of 1873 the town site had been created, and it ultimately would have a population of over 2,000. U.S. senators John P. Jones and William Stewart invested heavily in the community and surrounding mining operations. Panamint proved to be the first of many mining boomtowns that would be created in the Death Valley region. Darwin was next, in 1874, and was followed by Lookout, Modoc, and many others during the late 1890s and early 1900s.

The discovery of borax led to commercial production in Death Valley, first at the Eagle Borax Works by Isadore Daunet in 1882, and shortly thereafter by William Coleman at the Harmony Borax Works in 1883. Borax production led to various transportation systems used in the Death Valley area—the first and most famous of which were the 20-mule teams used at the Harmony Borax Works and later adopted as a company logo by the Pacific Coast Borax Company. F. M. "Borax" Smith first experimented with a traction engine and later built the Tidewater and Tonopah (T&T) Railroad and various feeder lines to transport the shipments of borax. Borax was also instrumental in the creation of the company town of Ryan as well as the construction of the Tidewater and Tonopah Railroad and the Death Valley Railroad, which transported the shipments of borax.

When gold was discovered at Bullfrog in 1904 by Death Valley prospector Shorty Harris and his partner Ed Cross, it helped usher in another prolific era of mining in Death Valley. This created a new series of boomtowns. The high price of copper added an impetus to the frenzy. The town-site promoters (who were also the mining promoters) would petition Washington for a post office, giving a glowing report of the area and the estimated population—both fictional. When the post office examiners ultimately determined that the town did not exist, the official post office would be rescinded without there being any activity, or town for that matter. Examples include Alakali, Donald, Furnace, Goldvalley, Keane Springs, and Neptune. Thereafter, towns were established sporadically for a variety of reasons. Keane Wonder served the mining center that grew around the Keane Wonder Mine. Leadfield was a town that was created in 1926 to promote and support a mining swindle.

In addition to mining activity, tourism has promoted the development of Death Valley. Tourists have been drawn to Death Valley ever since roads and transportation have been available (the roads and transportation owing their existence to mining). In 1926, H. W. "Bob" Eichbaum tried to capitalize on this by building a road from Darwin into Death Valley. His equipment got stuck at the old stovepipe well, and that is where he built his resort, Bungalette City, which is now known as Stovepipe Wells. To accommodate the growing number of tourists, the Pacific Coast Borax Company built a first-class facility called the Furnace Creek Inn at Furnace Creek in the late 1920s. More affordable accommodations were built at the Furnace Creek Ranch and at Panamint Springs in the 1930s. Scotty's Castle also provided lodging to a select number of people for a short period of time during the 1940s. And the Pacific Coast Borax Company converted their miners' dormitories to hotels at Death Valley Junction and at Ryan.

Death Valley has long held a fascination for visitors even before it had any tourist facilities. In addition to its catchy name, adding to its mystique was the shameless self-promotion of "Death Valley Scotty" for a period spanning over 50 years. When asked about Death Valley, most people will refer to Scotty, or Scotty's Castle, as the area's most recognizable icon. Scotty's Castle, a 25-room Spanish-style mansion, was built by Chicago insurance man Albert Johnson at a cost of over $2 million. While most people associate Death Valley Scotty with "his" castle, he was on the national scene as early as 1905, when he chartered a train to break the Chicago–Los Angeles speed record. Before his record-breaking run, Scotty was an undistinguished cowboy with Buffalo Bill's Wild West Show. Scotty was part con man, part showman, and part public-relations expert with a large dose of P. T. Barnum thrown in. He epitomizes Death Valley—a land of mystery, a land of dreams.

# One

# EARLY HISTORY
## PIONEERS, NATIVE INHABITANTS, AND BORAX

The popular history of man's occupation of Death Valley usually starts with the gold-seeking party of 1849, which made an ill-fated decision to take a shortcut to the California goldfields through Death Valley. This group split up into several smaller factions, each taking a different road. When they could go no further, two young men, William Manly and John Rogers, set out to find help. They made it to the pueblo of Los Angeles and returned to Death Valley, bringing lifesaving supplies and leading the rest of the party to safety.

Of course there is more to the story. Native inhabitants lived in Death Valley and the surrounding region for thousands of years before that first forty-niner party arrived. The early inhabitants of Death Valley are commonly divided into four periods: Nevares Spring People about 9,000 years ago; Mesquite Flat People about 5,000 years ago; Saratoga Spring People about 3,000 years ago; and Shoshone about 1,000 years ago. The Shoshone were ancestors of the present-day Timbisha Shoshone tribe (known as Panamint Shoshone until 2000, when the federal government gave recognition to the tribe). These native inhabitants were seminomadic and have not left much of a visual record.

After the original forty-niner party, Death Valley has been the site of many expeditions in search of mineral wealth. Silver and gold were the most sought, but it was the initial discovery of borax by Aaron and Rosie Winters that led to the first successful commercial development in Death Valley. Early efforts at the Eagle Borax Works and William T. Coleman's Harmony Borax Works failed after a few years. It was Francis M. "Borax" Smith who purchased Coleman's interests and formed the Pacific Coast Borax Company, which developed the Death Valley region. He built railroads to transport the borax ore and promoted the 20-mule team brand and logo in national advertising.

William Lewis Manly was an original member of the gold-seeking party that ended up crossing Death Valley in 1849 since they did not want to chance going through the Sierras during the winter. When his group could go no farther, Manly and John Rogers went to seek help. They made it to the pueblo of Los Angeles, then headed back to Death Valley to successfully rescue their party.

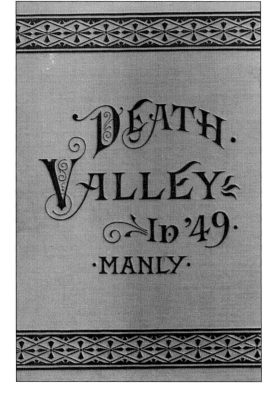

In 1894, Manly published the book *Death Valley in '49*, which was the first popular account of that fateful trip. Manly's heroic account did much to popularize and bring Death Valley to the attention of rest of the country. Manly Beacon, Manly Dome, Manly Fall, Manly Pass, and Lake Manly are all named for this book's author.

This is one of many reenactments of the original Death Valley forty-niner wagon trains that have been performed over the years (the original pioneers did not have cameras). The reenactments have been for promotional purposes for the Pacific Coast Borax Company, for the television series *Death Valley Days,* and for films shot in Death Valley and in connection with the annual Death Valley '49ers Encampment. This reenactment was done in the 1930s.

This map depicts the possible routes that the forty-niner parties took crossing Death Valley in 1849. The unbroken solid line shows the course the Manly-Bennett took through and out of Death Valley. This map was created in 1939 for Carl Wheat and its accuracy has been debated ever since. An exhaustive study of all routes can be found in *Escape from Death Valley* by Leroy and Jean Johnson.

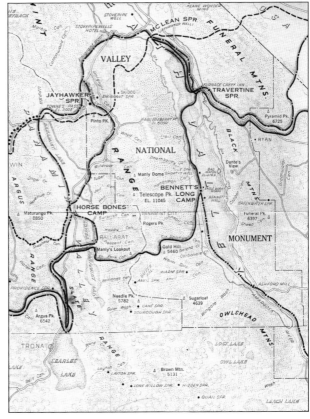

"Emigrant Camp, Death Valley, California, the place where the Jayhawker Party camped and their Oxen Perished in 1849. 110 feet below Sea Level" is shown in 1911. Darwin French entered Death Valley in May 1860 looking for the lost gunsight lead. His party came across this emigrant campsite and found wagons, yokes, guns, cooking utensils, and many other objects lying untouched.

A lone prospector can be seen working his claim at what was called the "Jay Hawkers last camp ground at Salt Creek Flat, 110 feet below sea level." In 1932, Bill and Edna Price dug up relics and sold them to tourists at this site, many years after this photograph was taken. It certainly is possible that some of the relics they sold were from this prospector's camp and not the Jayhawker party of 1849.

A stock certificate for 10 shares in the Jefferson Gold and Silver Mining Company provides evidence of very early organized mining activity in the Death Valley region. The mines for this company were located in the Slate Range District, which was formed in November 1861 by the Searles brothers, among others, during the mining excitement at Coso. The Slate Range was crossed by the Jayhawker party 12 years earlier on their way to Searles Lake out of Death Valley.

Johnny Shoshone is displaying a large rattlesnake used in a movie filmed in Death Valley called *Fangs of Death Valley*. Johnny Shoshone claimed to have seen the first white men enter Death Valley in 1849. The film is mentioned in the Lone Pine Film Museum database, but nothing other than its title is known about it.

This is one of the last photographs taken of "Shoshone Johnny," a cousin of "Indian George." Shoshone Johnny is credited along with Bob Montgomery as having located the claims that led to the economic development of Rhyolite in 1904. The Montgomery Shoshone Mine, named for Bob Montgomery and Shoshone Johnny, was the largest producer in the Bullfrog District. Shoshone Johnny was also known as "Hungry Johnny" and is sometimes referred to as "Johnny Shoshone." This confusion can be attributed to the fact that the Panamint Shoshone Indians did not adopt Western names until very late in the 18th century or early in the 19th century. Johnny was a favorite subject for photographs by visitors to Death Valley. He would pose for photographs at Furnace Creek until his death in 1953. (Photograph by Tom G. Murray.)

This photograph of Furnace Creek Ranch was taken in 1912. Furnace Creek Ranch, originally known as Greenland Ranch, was started by Borax man William T. Coleman at the mouth of Furnace Creek in the mid-1880s. The *Death Valley Chuck-Walla* newspaper referred to the buildings in this photograph as "The Hacienda at Furnace Creek."

Panamint Shoshone or Timbisha women are shown working at the Furnace Creek Indian Camp in the late 1920s, just after tourist facilities were being built and improved in Death Valley. This image illustrates the influence of the nonnative population on native culture. Metal pails and buckets and canvas tents are evident instead of the native baskets and grass houses. (Willard.)

Another example illustrating how quickly the descendants of the Timbisha Shoshone (the original inhabitants of Death Valley for the first 1,000 years) adapted to the "white man's ways." Shown here is a group of Shoshone Indians in their 1925 automobiles near Ryan. Note the modern clothes and riding cap.

A well-used road leading to Furnace Creek Ranch is clearly visible about 20 years after the 1912 photograph on page 15 was taken. More buildings and palm trees are in evidence. Today Furnace Creek Ranch is the name of the tourist complex near the Furnace Creek Inn. The Timbisha Shoshone still maintain a tribal village area near Furnace Creek Ranch. (Willard.)

The actual creek at Furnace Creek is visible in this 1892 image. The creek provided much-needed water for the native population. The largest Native American village in Death Valley was located at the mouth of Furnace Creek. The horse and buggy shown here was not used by the Native Americans at this time but was a means of local transportation for the benefit of the borax works nearby.

One of Hungry Bill's sons (on the right) can be seen standing in the middle of the main street in Darwin with Gunn's saloon in the background. Hungry Bill was best known for having made raids into San Bernardino and Los Angeles with his brother "Panamint Tom" during the 1870s to steal horses from the ranches.

Rhyolite photographer A. E. Holt took this photograph in 1905 of Native Americans gambling in Death Valley, near Beatty, Nevada. An early use of canvas as a housing material can be seen as compared to the more traditional grass and willow. Note the basket used as a hat by the woman at the far right. Beginning about 1920, baskets were made primarily for tourists.

On the back of this photograph the following is written: "Devil's Bake Oven in Amargosa, California. Indian burial grounds in foreground. Horse with a light mane in a tiny corral in midground. Mining camp in background." The mining camp was probably located near where the Amargosa Borax Works operated south of Shoshone during the 1880s. There was a short-lived town of Amargosa near Rhyolite, and all of its buildings were moved to Bullfrog.

"Indian George Hansen" (left) and "Shorty" Harris are having an animated conversation in the Panamint Valley in 1930. Indian George was born in 1841 and often related stories of seeing the first white men enter Death Valley in 1849. He also claimed he saw pioneer prospector Jacob Breyfogle twice near Stovepipe Wells.

This is another shot of pioneer Death Valley prospector Shorty Harris with Indian George at the Indian Ranch. The Indian Ranch was leased to the Barker family in the late 1960s. This left the Barkers' own ranch at the top of Goler Canyon vacant, enabling Charles Manson to use it as his hideout. Manson was arrested at this ranch.

As the borax mines started closing, the Panamint Shoshone Indians that were living and working in Death Valley started to work for Albert Johnson to help build Scotty's Castle. A hatless Death Valley Scotty is in the white shirt and tie (third from left of the dog), posing with some of these workers.

Native Americans are working on the fence at Scotty's Lower Vine Ranch. There are extensive records of Native Americans working on the castle from 1925 to 1931, and this photograph dates from that same time. Pete Cherooty was responsible for lining up the posts, and Maxfield was the supervisor.

Tatzumbie DuPea wrote on this photograph, "I was born in the year 1849 and was in Death Valley before the first white man." Her headstone reads, "Tatzumbie DuPea, Native Piute Indian, 1849–1970." At the time of her death, she was believed to be the oldest person buried at Forest Lawn. Unfortunately, this is not true. Elizabeth Mecham recalled that Tatzumbie attended grammar school with her in Darwin during the early 1900s. (Photograph by Tom G. Murray.)

Dobie Gunnarson built this stone monument to his friend Serafin Esteves who, with Gunnarson, did the rock work at Furnace Creek Inn. This monument is situated on top of a little rocky knoll a short distance to the south of the road that leads off the Texas Springs campground. The five graves at the site of this monument contain the remains of Native Americans who lived in Death Valley. (Photograph by Tom G. Murray.)

Philander "Phi" Lee is just barely discernable in front of the tree to the right of his home at Resting Spring. To the right of Philander is his brother Leander "Cub." The Lee brothers made the biggest borax discovery in Death Valley in 1882. Phi sold the claim and bought this ranch with the money. The claim later became the Lila C., the center of borax mining in the United States.

The Eagle Borax Works, shown here in 1892, is considered the first commercial borax operation in Death Valley. It was started by Isadore Daunet in 1881. The operations were located south in Death Valley near Bennetts Well. The Eagle Borax Works ceased production in 1884. Shortly thereafter, Daunet committed suicide.

The Harmony Borax Works were in ruins in the 1920s, when this photograph was taken. The Harmony Borax Mining Company was a successful borax producer in Death Valley during the 1880s. Owned by F. M. "Borax" Smith and operated by William T. Coleman, it produced about two million pounds of borax a year until the price of borax dropped from 15¢ a pound to under 6¢ in 1887. The operations closed in May 1888. (Willard.)

This commercial photograph, titled "Old Borax Wagons at Furnace Creek," was sold to tourists about 1930. It is difficult to determine from this perspective that the original 20-mule team wagons built for the Pacific Coast Borax Company were huge, with 7-foot high rear wheels and 5-foot high front wheels. The wagons could carry over 10 tons of borax. (Willard.)

Johnnie O'Keefe (left) was one of the last survivors of the original 20-mule team skinners. His unidentified companion was a swamper when the Pacific Coast Borax Company reactivated the team in 1936 for the dedication of the Golden Gate Bridge. O'Keefe was featured in a 1938 radio episode of *Death Valley Days*. (Photograph by Tom G. Murray.)

From left to right, Belle Hutchinson, Gertrude Saunders, Alex Isgallor (?), Jerome Connelly, and Walter Saunders are identified as being the passengers on this trip of "Old Dinah," the traction engine originally brought to Death Valley by Borax Smith to haul borax ore from the Pacific Coast Borax Company mines. The engine frequently got stuck, which led Smith to build the Tonopah and Tidewater Railroad.

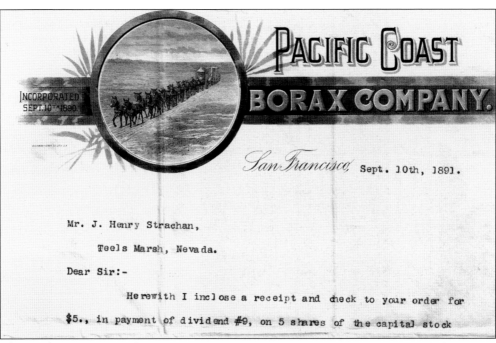

The Pacific Coast Borax Company started using the 20-mule team as the company logo in 1891. The 1891 letter is addressed to J. Henry Strachan, who was the superintendent of the Teel's Marsh Borax Works and who was also a stockholder in the Pacific Coast Borax Company, which ultimately ended up as owner of the Teel's Marsh borax properties.

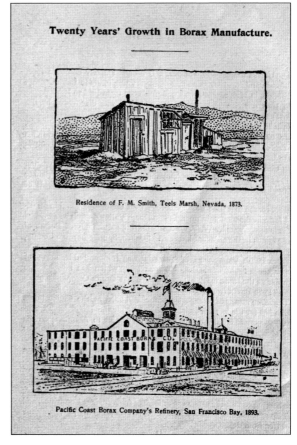

Twenty Years' Growth in Borax Manufacture.

Residence of F. M. Smith, Teels Marsh, Nevada, 1873.

Pacific Coast Borax Company's Refinery, San Francisco Bay, 1893.

These simple pictures, contained in an 1895 advertising brochure, illustrate the growth in the production of borax by the Pacific Coast Borax Company. The wooden shack was the home of Francis M. "Borax" Smith before he began the development and production of the Death Valley mineral that would make his fame and fortune.

This is a photograph of Death Valley graves near Eagle Borax. These unmarked Death Valley graves may be those of unknown early pioneers. They could also be the graves of some of the estimated 15 to 35 men who died in Death Valley during the summer of 1905. There have been over 100 deaths in Death Valley due to dehydration and thirst. (Willard.)

This photograph of Death Valley graves was taken by Zane Grey during his trip to Death Valley in 1919. Grey and his companion wanted to walk the seven miles across Death Valley but were advised against it. They made the walk anyway, and after the arduous trek, Grey was inspired to write a magazine article, a short story, and the novel *Wanderer of the Wasteland*.

This is a typical prospector on the floor of Death Valley, said to be John Lemoigne with his burros. Lemoigne, like many of his contemporaries in Death Valley, would not prospect where others would expect to find good ore but rather went places others feared. The Death Valley prospector usually was secretive, and many were accompanied by a burro or two to assist in transport. Lemoigne perished in Death Valley in 1919. At age 77, he was found dead under a mesquite bush with his burros. There still is a controversy whether Death Valley Scotty or Frank Crampton and Shorty Harris discovered Lemoigne's body.

Val Nolan was a prospector and a frequent visitor at Stove Pipe Wells Hotel. A Mr. Cooper, a guest at the hotel, told Bob Eichbaum, the owner, that there was a dead man not far away. It was Bob Eichbaum and Mr. Cooper from New York who dug the grave and buried Nolan where he was found. J. A. Hunter (left) and Clarence Harcourt, both of Stovepipe Wells, are shown building a prospector's monument of stones over the grave in 1932.

James Dayton was the caretaker at Furnace Creek Ranch after the Harmony Borax Company mines closed. He died when he tried to travel to Daggett in the heat of summer and was buried where he fell. His fame derives solely from his picturesque grave, which was often photographed with bones. The gravesite was changed in 1936 when Shorty Harris was buried beside Dayton and a monument erected. (Photograph by Steve Danish.)

The caption on this photograph is "Dry Canyon Furnace Valley near Death Valley Ca. where you find a few bleached human bones which will explain the historic journey in early days." This photograph was taken in 1907 by Per Larson. Larson was known as Larss when he took photographs with Ducloss in the Klondike during the Alaska gold rush.

Author Ralph Paine wrote the following on the back of this photograph: "Old Man Crump a battered soldier of fortune, Taken April 5, 1906." Bill Crump was featured in two of Paine's books, *The Greater America* and *Roads of Adventure*. Crump was a stage driver and miner. He entered the Death Valley area with a government-sponsored surveying expedition. Crump told Paine that he was a stage driver only until he could head back to Alaska to look for gold.

Death Valley has never been the exclusive province of men. A woman identified as "Della," dressed in all her finery, poses for this early photograph next to her tent. The location of the camp in this photograph is given by Della as "The Funeral Range of Mountains on the border of Death Valley, California."

Mary Elizabeth White, known as "Panamint Annie," was one of a few female prospectors in Death Valley before World War II. She is shown here in back of the Borax Museum in Furnace Creek Ranch standing next to the printing press used to print Greenwater's newspaper the *Death Valley Chuck-Walla*. (Photograph by Tom G. Murray.)

# Two

# PROSPECTORS, MINING, AND TRANSPORTATION

Mining in Death Valley has taken place ever since 1849 when the first forty-niner party entered the valley looking for a shortcut to the California goldfields. After the initial party made it out, little time was lost in organizing prospecting parties to search for mineral wealth, and prospectors have crisscrossed the Death Valley area, including those parties led by Erasmus Darwin French (for whom Darwin Falls and the town of Darwin are named) and S. G. George.

Death Valley has had its share of colorful characters. These include a number of mining men about which many tall tales have been told—some of them even true. The most colorful are about Shorty Harris and "Seldom Seen Slim," both of whom spent most of their lives in the area, died, and are buried there as well. Most famous of all was Death Valley Scotty, who will be discussed in greater detail in chapter four.

Prospecting in the Death Valley area with its harsh conditions to find a mineral deposit that could be developed commercially was only part of the problem. Even if a mineral deposit could be found, transporting the ore over the long distances to milling facilities, processing plants, and ultimately to the markets was an additional challenge. The initial solution to this transportation problem was the use of the 20-mule teams. It was soon determined that improvements on this time-consuming trek from the borax deposits in Death Valley to the railroad at Mojave were needed. Necessity led to a number of innovative solutions, including the steam-traction engine "Old Dinah" and a monorail covering a distance of 28 miles, neither of which was particularly successful. Ultimately railroads and spur lines were found to be the best method of transport. These included the Tonopah and Tidewater Railroad, Bullfrog Goldfield Railroad, Las Vegas and Tonopah Railroad (whose depot is one of the few remaining buildings in Rhyolite), Tecopa Railroad, and Death Valley Railroad.

Written on this photograph of prospectors at Bennetts Hole is the following: "We have claims near here. To the left is where Death Valley Scotty had his supposed rich ore. The fellow feeding the burro once cornered the cotton market finally, lost and then was sent in this country to get track of Scotty's mines." The man mentioned could be one of the men Julian M. Gerrard hired to find out the truth about Scotty's rich mine, which Gerrard had grubstaked to the tune of $10,000 from 1902 to 1905.

Bill Keyes is camping with a friend at the mouth of Willow Creek in Death Valley in 1906. Keyes was an early Death Valley prospector who had some success with viable mines. Keyes was an early ally of Death Valley Scotty and provided Scotty with the use of his mines to give credence to Scotty's claims to prospective investors.

The copper frenzy of 1906 led to a mining stampede at Greenwater in Death Valley. Mining promoters quickly staked locations and sold stock, and the town of Greenwater grew overnight. Shown are three prospectors looking somewhat dejected at their mine in Greenwater in February 1907. The town did not survive for much longer after this picture was taken.

GRAND OPENING BALL
GIVEN BY
BEATTY MINERS UNION NO. 245 W. F. M.
BEATTY, NEVADA

MONDAY NIGHT, APRIL 1st, 1907

BEST OF MUSIC
TICKETS $1.50
LADIES FREE          ADMIT ONE

Pictured is an admission ticket to the Grand Opening Ball of the Beatty Miners Union, April 14, 1907. Mining was hard work and a necessary part of any miners' union was to provide for the entertainment of its members. Social events, such as this ball, were a diversion from the normal saloons, brothels, and opium dens that competed for the miners' hard-earned dollars.

The Keane Wonder Mine and mill is pictured here. The mine was located in the Bullfrog mining district, about 22 miles south of Rhyolite. A town developed around the mining camp and had a post office from 1912 to 1914. The mine and the town were named for Jack Keane, who was its codiscoverer with Domingo Etcharren. (NPS photograph.)

Domingo Etcharren, "the one-eyed Basque," discovered the Keane Wonder Mine with Jack Keane. Etcharren sold his half of the Keane Wonder for $25,000 and used the money to start a butcher business in Ballarat and buy a store, land, and houses in Darwin. He is buried in the Darwin cemetery.

This is the earliest known photograph of Shorty Harris. Shorty was known to have prospected in both Tombstone and Death Valley after having worked underground in the Darwin mines in the 1870s. He is credited with the discovery of Bullfrog in Nevada and Harrisburg in Death Valley. He also claimed to have made the original discovery at Greenwater, but his partner failed to record the claims.

The graves of Shorty Harris and James Dayton have Shorty's words recorded on the marker. They read, "Bury me beside Jim Dayton in the valley we loved above me write: 'Here lies Shorty Harris, a single blanket jackass prospector.'—Epitaph requested by Shorty (Frank) Harris beloved gold hunter. 1856-1934. Here Jas. Dayton, pioneer, perished, 1898."

The men in this photograph are identified on the back as "Lee Fergus, Shattuck and (Ralph J. "Dad") Fairbanks at ranch." It was probably taken at Fairbanks's ranch in Ash Fork. Dad Fairbanks ran the last store and saloon in Greenwater, the Furnace Mercantile. He left Greenwater and took all of its remaining buildings to found the town of Shoshone in 1910.

This is the Tonopah and Tidewater Railroad water tower at Shoshone. An eating stop was established for the Tonopah and Tidewater Railroad at Shoshone in about 1910, and it was run by Ralph J. "Dad" Fairbanks. This photograph was taken in 1934. (Photograph by George J. Capdevielle.)

"Freighting to Panamint" describes this scene of a pack train getting ready to head to the new mining boomtown of Panamint. Death Valley was isolated from major supply centers, so materials had to be imported from great distances to build houses, mills, stores, and even towns that boasted populations of thousands of people.

113.   Freighting t  Panamint.

Patrick Reddy, the one-armed gunfighter turned lawyer, was the dominant force in the Death Valley legal community from the early 1870s in Panamint until his death in 1900. He was a state senator for the Death Valley region and owned the largest producing silver mine in the area as well—the Defiance Mine, located in Darwin. (Courtesy of Eastern California Museum.)

"A stage station near Death Valley" is written by author Ralph D. Paine on the back of this photograph, taken in 1906. A "stage" usually conjures up the image of a Concord coach; however, as can be seen from the wagons and buggy in this photograph, stage had a different connotation in Death Valley. Later the definition of stage included auto coaches and even buses.

Luciano Gagliano (right) was one of the few Italian mule-team drivers in the Death Valley region at the beginning of the 20th century. After advent of the railroad, the use of mule teams declined in the area and Gagliano, like many of his freighting comrades in Death Valley, became a teamster in Southern California.

Seen is a prospector with his burros leaving the Trading Post in Tecopa after coming into town to get provisions for his next prospecting trip. Tecopa was a short-lived, 1870s mining town that was twice resurrected and was the largest silver-lead producer in California in 1917.

This photograph shows the Tecopa Railroad Company's Engine No. 1 at the loader. Mickey Devine is the engineer in the engine's cab. The Tecopa Railroad was built primarily to service the Noonday Mine and a two-mile branch was subsequently built to the Gunsight Mine.

The Tecopa Mercantile is the store where Henry P. "Harry" Stimler was shot and killed by its proprietor Franklin A. Hall on August 22, 1931. After killing Stimler with no apparent motive, Hall shot and killed himself. Harry Stimler and William Marsh are credited with the discovery and founding of Goldfield in 1902.

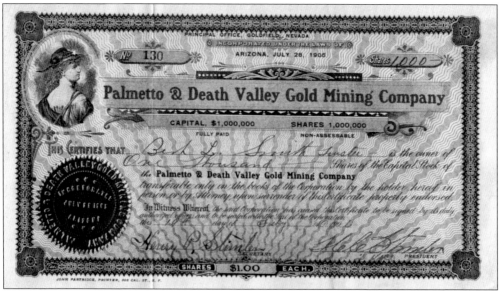

Seen here is a stock certificate for 1,000 shares in the Palmetto and Death Valley Gold Mining Company, which was formed by Harry Stimler and his brother when the discovery of ore assaying $20,000 a ton reopened the Palmetto rush of 1866. The discovery brought 600 miners to the area in early 1906. The certificate is signed by both Stimler brothers.

Written on the back of this photograph is the following: "Emery Bodge perished in Death Valley 1908 in August with his pal Tommy Flos this is just as they found him reading from left to right: Frank Thessie, Dr. McDonald, Frank Pfluger, Jack Casey, Jim O'Conley, Frank Kennedy, Henry Sellers, Dick Hibberd, all from Skidoo." The photograph was taken by the party that left Skidoo to retrieve the bodies of Emory Bodge and Thomas Flause, who foolishly left Rhyolite for Skidoo on foot in the middle of August.

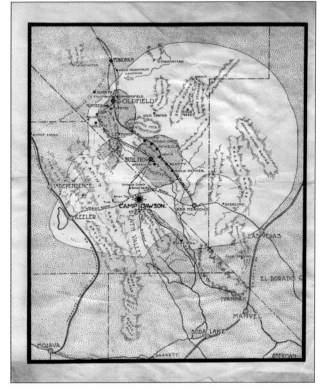

This is a promotional map (in the shape of a skull) made by B. X. Dawson for "Camp Dawson," a fictional mining camp south of Furnace Creek in Death Valley created to fleece investors during the mining boom of 1905–1906. Dawson claimed to have found prehistoric mining tools in the area and formed the Death Valley Gold Mining and Milling Company to capitalize on it.

William M. Stewart, U.S. senator, prominent mining attorney, and co-financier of Panamint, returned to Death Valley in 1905 to open a law office and to make his home in Bullfrog. Stewart left Bullfrog in 1908. Like many other Death Valley lawyers and lawmen, Stewart went to Tombstone, Arizona, in the early 1880s. While there, Stewart was an eyewitness to the gunfight at the OK Corral.

"Lunch in Death Valley. Foot of Ibex Wash. Bob Montgomery, Sam Yount and Shattuck," is written on the back of this photograph. Bob Montgomery is best known as the discoverer of the Montgomery Shoshone Mine in the Bullfrog District, which put Rhyolite on the map. Previously he discovered the Oh Be Joyful Mine in Ballarat, and he later purchased the Gold Eagle claims in Skidoo. Sam Yount was a 20-mule team driver in Death Valley and owned a copper mine at Goodsprings in 1900.

This is an early photograph of the office and boardinghouse at the Lucky Jim Mine located in the New Coso Mining District. The Lucky Jim has been producing silver lead ore since 1875 for a number of different owners, including George Hearst. Although a fire in 1928 shut it down for 20 years, it subsequently reopened and has produced off and on ever since.

Ten charcoal kilns were built in Wildrose Canyon by George Hearst in 1877 to supply charcoal for the smelters of the Modock Consolidated Mining Company, located 25 miles away. Each kiln is a little over 25 feet high and has a circumference of over 30 feet. To produce the charcoal, the kilns burned pinyon pines, which could be found nearby.

Burros are not native to Death Valley but were introduced by miners who later either left the area or died and abandoned them. The burros adapted and prospered. During the 1980s, the National Park Service embarked on a program to remove them all since they are not native to Death Valley (of course, neither is man). The program was successful, but occasionally, some can still be seen running wild today.

"Seldom Seen Slim" (Charles Ferge) is seen with his corncob pipe and the Panamint Mountains in the background. A popular "desert rat" long a favorite with Death Valley visitors, Slim was in the later wave of Death Valley prospectors. He arrived in Ballarat about 1913 or so and was a fixture there until his death in 1968. Slim is buried in the Ballarat cemetery, and Slim's Peak in the Panamint range was named for him. (Photograph by Tom G. Murray.)

Shorty Harris (left) and Jim Sherlock are pictured at Ballarat. Jim Sherlock was guarded about his past, which may have included a stint as a gambler and gunfighter in Montana and Wyoming. He is best known for outwitting local gamblers in 1903 by driving a buggy with a team of burros to beat the speed record from Ballarat to Los Angeles, previously set by a team of fast horses.

This is Shorty Harris showing ore to prospective investors at Ballarat. Shorty was a fixture in Death Valley for many years and liked to be known as the last of the single blanket jackass prospectors. Unlike many prospectors, Shorty made several noteworthy discoveries; however, he always sold out too soon and drank away his profits.

Bill Shaw (left), Tommy Thompson (center), and Louie Bloom are shown at Rhyolite in 1938 and represent the typical Death Valley prospectors of the 1930s. Little had changed in prospecting methods or prospector appearance for over 70 years. Years after this photograph was taken, Thompson moved into and lived in the Rhyolite Bottle House.

This dugout near Stovepipe Wells is the remains of a stage stop on the road between Rhyolite and Skidoo in the early 1900s and was used as a refreshment stand. Built by James Clark, it was known as the Stovepipe Road House. It is often referred to as the "First Stove Pipe Wells Hotel" or Death Valley's first "resort." This photograph was taken in the 1930s as the dugout began to slowly melt into the desert.

This Tonopah and Tidewater Railroad car was used as an office at the head of the line during construction of a 200-mile railroad line from Ludlow, California, to Beatty, Nevada, to haul borax deposits owned by Borax Smith. The photograph was taken at Death Valley Junction in 1907.

This is a map of the Tonopah and Tidewater Railroad showing all the stations in Death Valley and surrounding regions. This map is on the back of a Tonopah and Tidewater Company letter dated 1912. The Tonopah and Tidewater Company was the result of a 1908 merger between the Tonopah and Tidewater Railroad and the Bullfrog Goldfield Railroad.

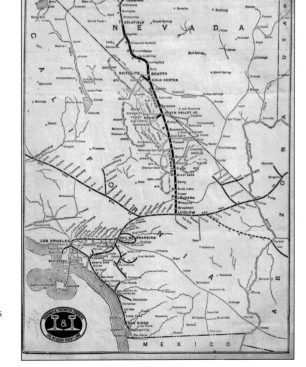

A. Lockhurst is shown riding the "Widow Train" in Ryan. The Widow Train was the Ryan narrow-gauge railroad used to transport borax and was named for the Widow Mine near Ryan. This photograph is unusual since it shows the train being used for its original purpose, transporting borax.

After the mines closed down in Ryan, the Pacific Coast Borax Company converted the town and some of its buildings to accommodate Death Valley visitors. This photograph shows how the train that was originally used for mining purposes was reconfigured to provide pleasure excursions for tourists. During its operation, it remained a popular photo opportunity. (Willard.)

Capt. Ray A. Gibson is standing next to one of the borax wagons he may have driven in his youth. Gibson is known as "the last of the Death Valley teamsters." Gibson came to the Death Valley area in about 1899 and served as a commissary man and a chainman on the railroad before getting a job as a swamper on a freight team with 16 horses, not 20 mules. (Photograph by Tom G. Murray.)

Death Valley actually had its own monorail decades before Disneyland. The monorail was built to transport Epsom salts 28 miles from the deposits in Crystal Hills, across Layton Canyon and Wingate Pass to the Trona Railroad at Searles. It shortened the 63-mile truck route and went through twisting, steep canyons that a narrow-gauge railroad could not. Conceived in 1918 by Thomas Wright, president of American Magnesium Company, the monorail was finally completed in 1924.

From left to right, Frank Tilton, W. H. "Brownie" Brown, and Sy Johnson are shown in this photograph, taken at the Death Valley Junction station on June 15, 1940, the last day of the operation of the Tonopah and Tidewater Railroad. Frank Tilton was best known for giving James Dayton his last rites after Tilton and Adolph Nevares found and buried him.

Written on the back of this photograph is "First car to go into Death Valley." If this statement is accurate, the car would either be the one driven by Malcolm Macdonald to the edge of Death Valley in 1905 or the one Larry Sullivan, Jack Campbell, and James Hopper drove to Emigrant Spring in 1906. The car is sitting in front of the Pacific Coast Borax Company complex at Death Valley Junction.

# Three

# BOOMTOWNS

The Death Valley region was home to its share of boomtowns—towns that went through a boom and bust cycle primarily due to mining activity. A discovery would be made; a mining district formed; prospectors and miners would flood to the area; tents, cabins, and more substantial structures would be built; stores and services would be offered; sometimes a newspaper would be printed; and of course there would be a proliferation of saloons, usually at least one saloon per every 100 people. Promoters would raise capital, the towns would prosper, and sometimes ore would be processed and sold. When the discoveries proved illusory or mines failed to produce in commercial quantities, the prospectors and miners would leave, the stores would close, and the towns disappeared.

The earliest of these events occurred during the 1870s with the silver excitements in Panamint, Darwin, and Lookout. In the 1880s, borax mining was in force, but no towns grew as a result. The peak period for boomtowns in Death Valley would be from about 1900 to 1909. These were primarily due at first to the gold discoveries in Ballarat, Bullfrog, Rhyolite, and surrounding areas and a bit later from copper as well. Towns that were established a bit later in this period included Alkali, Death Valley, Donald, Furnace, Goldvalley, Greenwater, Hoveck, Keane Springs, Lee, Neptune, Ryan, Schwab, and Skidoo. Many of these towns existed for only a year or two. They boomed and then busted after the market crash of 1907, with the fleeing population leaving them ghosts. The mining promoters created so many companies that the total capitalization for the Greenwater area alone was over a quarter of a billion dollars. When the crash came and the dust settled, it turned out that some of these 1906–1909 towns existed only on paper and the total production was miniscule.

In addition to the mining towns, other towns grew around stops on the various railroads that served the mining interests in Death Valley. Typically these towns also had a Wells Fargo office and a U.S. Post Office. Examples include Zabriskie, Death Valley Junction, Shoshone, and Beatty.

This view of the town of Rhyolite was taken in early December 1906. The discovery that led to the founding of Rhyolite was made by Shorty Harris and Ed Cross in 1904. The town grew quickly from canvas tents to substantial stone and brick buildings. The Montgomery Shoshone Mine was Rhyolite's largest producer.

"I am in the big mining district of the world" is written on the back of this photograph of Rhyolite, taken in 1909. By 1909, Rhyolite was a full-fledged city bustling with an estimated population of up to 10,000 (although 5,000–6,000 is more likely). The full extent of the city can be seen here. This is in stark contrast to the present-day ghost town of Rhyolite on the edge of Death Valley, where only the train depot, restored bottle house, and a few other skeletal structures remain.

This cyanotype photograph of the famous bottle house in Rhyolite was taken by A. E. Holt in 1906, when the bottle house was first built by Tom Kelly. The Bennett family was its first occupants. The little girl sitting on the porch is Maxine Woolever (née Bennett), who became a photographer in Hollywood.

This photograph was taken by Rhyolite photographer A. E. Holt and shows the miners' union in a parade on Rhyolite's main street on February 17, 1907. At this time, Rhyolite was still in the midst of its building boom and not all of the major buildings had been completed.

"A city street in the Bullfrog District" is written on the back of this photograph by Ralph D. Paine, which was taken in 1906. At this time, the Bullfrog District would have included the towns of Bullfrog, Rhyolite, Gold Center, South Bullfrog, and Amargosa, which were very close to one another and whose boundaries were not exact. Gold Bar, Beatty, and possibly Johnnie (among others) were also in the district.

A sign for the short-lived town of Cuprite can be seen in the background of this photograph taken in the spring of 1906. By late 1906, a station on the Bullfrog and Goldfield Railroad had been built at Cuprite, and a post office was established in 1907. In 1907, the *Death Valley Chuck-Walla* reported that promoter Parmenter Kent was trying to lure investors away from Greenwater to Cuprite.

Beatty, Nevada's, main street is shown in December 1906. The Mayflower Club, Ohio Café and Bakery, and The Northern can all be seen. Beatty was the transportation and supply center for the entire surrounding district. It was the southern terminus of the Bullfrog Goldfield Railroad and the northern terminus of the Tonopah and Tidewater Railroad. Today Beatty serves as the northeast entrance to Death Valley.

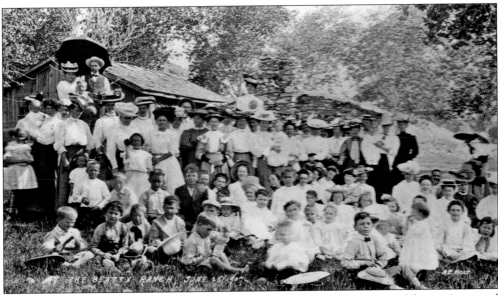

The town of Beatty was named for Montillus Murray "Old Man" Beatty, one of the area's original settlers. Many of Beatty's residents showed up for an outing at the Beatty ranch and posed for Rhyolite photographer A. E. Holt on June 25, 1907.

This view of Bullfrog, Nevada, at the edge of Death Valley was taken in early December 1906. At the time this photograph was taken, the rivalry between Rhyolite and Bullfrog for dominance over the Bullfrog District had ended with Rhyolite as the victor. Bullfrog stayed alive until the collapse of the district in 1909.

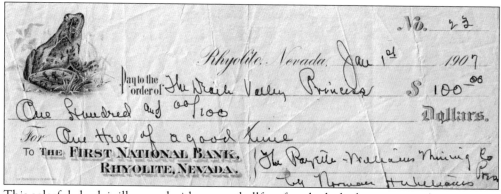

This colorful check is illustrated with a green bullfrog for which the large mining district on the edge of Death Valley was named. The ore that was discovered had a greenish hue similar to that of a bullfrog. Note the check was made payable to The Death Valley Princess for "One Hell of a good time" on New Year's Day, January 1, 1907.

"Hauling lumber to Bullfrog District '06" is written on the back of this photograph. Despite the inhospitable climate and harsh conditions, the mining frenzy caused towns to spring up in the unforgiving desert. Wood and other building materials had to be brought in from other areas. This photograph demonstrates how lumber was brought across the desert into the Death Valley area.

The Panamint Greenwater Gold and Copper Mining Company was one of hundreds of mining companies formed in the Death Valley region during 1906 and 1907 to capitalize on the speculative frenzy caused by rising copper prices. Almost none of the mines produced anything at all, and investors lost millions of dollars. This company tried to exploit the name of the old mining camp of Panamint to add luster to the new camp of Greenwater.

Panamint City was the first substantial town that was built in the Death Valley region. The Surprise Valley Mill, shown here, was owned by Sens. John P. Jones and William F. Stewart. It ran around the clock, processing about 15 tons of ore per day with a value of about $1,300.

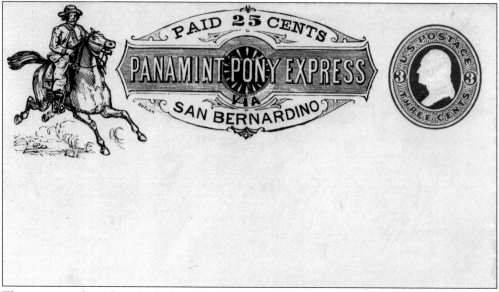

This is a prepaid envelope for the Panamint Pony Express. The Panamint Pony Express carried mail from Panamint City to San Bernardino and operated in 1874 and 1875. It also had a stop in Darwin. The express was owned by Panamint's largest employer, the Surprise Valley Mining Company. The only known rider was Philip Ross. (Courtesy of Robert Varlotta.)

There is widely held belief that the town of Panamint was wiped out in a flood in July 1876. This is not true. Panamint's post office was still doing a brisk business in 1877, and the records for the Surprise Valley Mill and Water Company show significant activity in 1877 as well. The mill in this picture did suffer damage from a major fire, which certainly helped speed Panamint's demise.

Located only a few miles from the current Death Valley National Park boundary, the mining town of Darwin (shown here in 1886) boomed in 1874 and was bust by 1879. It has been documented as one of the most violent towns in the 19th-century West. When the boom ended, many Darwin residents followed its newspaper to Bodie, and others, including gunmen and lawyers, went to Tombstone and figured prominently in the gunfight at the OK Corral. (Courtesy of Eastern California Museum.)

Unlike most of the Death Valley boomtowns, Darwin did not die, although it looks lifeless in this 1908 photograph. Sporadic mining activity kept it alive until 1926, when the Eichbaum toll road was built from Darwin to Death Valley and enabled Darwin to become a tourist town. State Route 190 opened in 1937, and it bypassed Darwin; however, during World War II, Darwin became a major supplier of lead. Darwin still clings to life today, with about 35 residents and a post office but no other services whatsoever.

The pioneer cemetery in Darwin contains the remains of many Death Valley notables, including Domingo Etcharren (codiscoverer of the Keane Wonder Mine); Nancy Williams (murder victim and madam); famed Panamint Shoshone Indian basket makers Mamie Gregory and Mary Wrinkle; and Wells Fargo stage robbery victim Jack T. Lloyd.

The July 4, 1907, drilling contest in Goldfield was a well-attended event. This photograph gives an idea of the huge population in the area during this boom period. The winners of the contest drilled a 40-inch hole in 15 minutes and won a prize of $900. Part of the sign for Tex Rickard's famed Northern Saloon can be seen in the left foreground.

The mining town of Goldfield grew quickly until the market crash of 1907 put a damper on growth. This photograph captures the 1907 Labor Day festivities in Goldfield. The handwritten caption reads, "Kangaroo Court where you get pinched and have to pay $1.00 to get out." The proceeds went to the Goldfield Fire Department.

Diamondfield, shown here in 1907, was founded in 1903 by "Diamondfield Jack" Davis, a noted gunfighter who had just been pardoned by the governor of Idaho for murder. Touted as being a rival to Goldfield, Diamondfield's fortune never materialized. By the end of 1904, Diamondfield had a post office and the usual saloons and other mining camp businesses. The post office closed in 1908 and with it went Diamondfield.

The short-lived mining boomtown of Schwab, here seen in ruins, was located in Echo Canyon. By early 1907, Schwab had a post office, telephone service, and a stage line. Its fame largely rests on the fact it was known as "A Mining Camp Built by Ladies" when three women—Mrs. F. W. Dunn, Gertrude Fessler, and Helen H. Black—took control of the town.

The town of Lookout was formed in 1875 and consisted of several stores, a number of buildings, and enough saloons to keep the local populace happy. While Lookout was not as violent as its contemporaries Darwin—its nearest neighbor—and Panamint, Lookout did have its share of gunfights, most notably the shooting of Augustine Moran by Constable Frank Fitzgerald; the shooting of Jack McGinnis by Oliver Roberts; and the gunfight that pitted Roberts and Fitzgerald against Dickey and Shay.

The remains of the rock foundation for the store at Lookout can be seen in this 1950 photograph. The view is looking west into the heart of the Argus mountains. The town of Darwin, Lookout's 1870s contemporary "sister city," is on the other side of the Argus range.

The Argenta mining camp in Death Valley was located near Aguereberry Point. In 1908, Dan Driscoll filed the first claim, although there are conflicting reports of ownership. In any event, George C. Griest took over ownership in 1929 or 1930 and was living there in 1933. Griest, known as "Sheriff of the Panamints," owned it until 1968. The Argenta Mine produced lead, silver, and zinc.

George Griest, known as "Silent George," was a deputy sheriff in Death Valley in the early 1930s. He is most known for the role he played in apprehending Jimmy Clebourne, who shot and killed Ed McSperrin in Wildrose Canyon on July 17, 1932. Griest lived at his Argenta Mine above Wildrose Station until his death in 1968.

Bunkhouse No. 1, built for the miners at Ryan, is in the right foreground of this photograph. Some of Ryan's residences are nearby, as is the telephone line. The south-central Death Valley route is in the middle of this photograph, just down from these buildings. The southernmost peak in the Greenwater range has been called "Chocolate Sundae Mountain" and is marked with an "X."

The town of Ryan was originally located at the Lila C. Mine, about seven miles southwest of Death Valley Junction. About 1915, the Lila C. ore deposits were running out and the buildings were moved to the Biddy McCarthy deposit about 12 miles to the northwest. Originally named Devar, the post office did not agree and reinstated the Ryan name for this new town. (Willard.)

Miners at the Biddy McCarthy Mine lounge in front of the company's store at "new Ryan" in 1925. The store building was built about 1915, when the town's other buildings were being moved from "old Ryan." Ryan never had a population that was much over 250. The mines in Ryan were closed at the end of 1927.

This swimming pool was called the "Travertino" by the miners at Ryan. The pool was fed by Travertine springs and served the miners, employees, and their families. These springs were also the source for a later swimming pool built to serve the upscale Furnace Creek Inn.

The last building in Greenwater is next to a porcelain road sign that was erected by the Automobile Club of Southern California about 1918 or so. Despite stock offerings that attempted to raise capital totaling over $250 million, very little ore was produced in Greenwater (total value about $2,600) and the town died after a short life. All of Greenwater's buildings were taken to build the town of Shoshone.

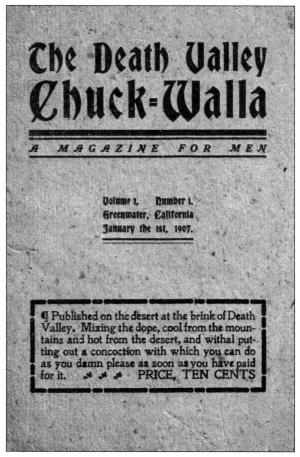

# The Death Valley Chuck-Walla

A MAGAZINE FOR MEN

Volume 1,   Number 1.
Greenwater, California
January the 1st, 1907.

¶ Published on the desert at the brink of Death Valley. Mixing the dope, cool from the mountains and hot from the desert, and withal putting out a concoction with which you can do as you damn please as soon as you have paid for it. ✻ ✻ ✻   PRICE, TEN CENTS

This first issue of Greenwater's newspaper, the *Death Valley Chuck-Walla*, was printed on butcher paper. Its entertaining writing style became somewhat famous, despite being a shameless booster of Greenwater and its mines. The printing press that printed this newspaper can be seen today outside the Borax Museum in Furnace Ranch.

By the 1920s, when this photograph was taken, the wild mining camps of Death Valley had settled down. Miners could now live with their wives and children in peace. Here one-half of the women's Death Valley baseball team is shown. They were based in the Pacific Coast Borax Company town of Ryan.

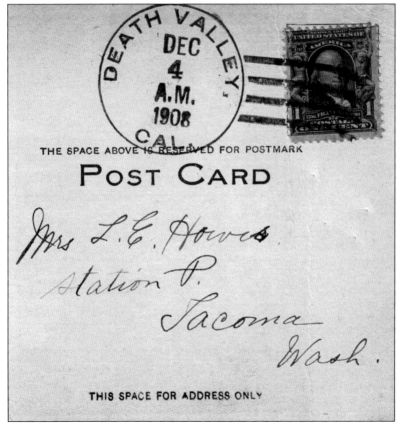

This postal cancellation is the earliest known from the Death Valley post office. In 1908, the post office was located at the Tonopah and Tidewater Railroad stop at Death Valley Junction. The Post Office Department shortened the name to Death Valley. Death Valley's first postmaster was Robert M. Tubb, who served from 1908 to 1912 but was better known for operating a brothel.

Taken about 1924, this may be the only known image of Russell's Camp, located two miles west of Ryan. W. Scott Russell staked some borax claims in Furnace Creek Wash, and when he went to record them, found out that United States Borax never perfected its title to the Clara, a profitable claim. Russell subsequently restaked it and obtained legal title. It was the subject of a number of lawsuits, but Russell ultimately prevailed.

Chloride City was the name of the mining camp located in the Chloride Cliff Mining District on the edge of Death Valley. Its heyday was during the Bullfrog mining excitement, from 1905 to 1907. It was built on the site of earlier mining activity in the 1870s.

Skidoo was another Death Valley mining town that came into existence in 1906. It lasted until 1917, longer than most of the others. Bob Montgomery, the founder of Rhyolite, was the driving force behind Skidoo. Unlike many of the other Death Valley boomtowns, Skidoo did generate revenue, about $1.5 million. At its peak, Skidoo had a population of about 700 with a post office, a newspaper, and a telegraph. This photograph was taken at the end of 1907 or the beginning of 1908.

Cy K. Babcock with a holstered gun stands in the doorway of the Skidoo Mining Company administration building in 1931. A 1927 Master Brougham Buick can be seen to the right of the photograph. Babcock operated the Wildrose Station and liked to be called "The Wildrose Kid."

Skidoo still had some buildings remaining in 1953, when this photograph was taken. Today all that can be seen are a couple of foundations and traces of the main road that went through the town. Its unusual name is said to derive from the popular expression of the day "23 Skidoo" and the fact that the nearest water was 23 miles away. Skidoo is best remembered for the lynching of Joe "Hootch" Simpson for the murder of Jim Arnold in 1908.

VOTE FOR... AND RE-ELECT

## CHAS. BROWN
(INCUMBENT)

## STATE SENATOR
Inyo-Mono-Alpine Counties ·

•

### EXPERIENCE! · SENIORITY!
**CONSCIENTIOUS REPRESENTATION OF THIS AREA FOR THE PAST 20 YEARS**

•

**Your Continued Support Respectfully Solicited**

*Chalfant Press*

Charles Brown was the sheriff of Greenwater during its 1906–1907 boom period. He then moved to Shoshone and started a hotel with his father-in-law, Ralph J. "Dad" Fairbanks. Brown became a well-respected state senator, representing the Death Valley area in Sacramento for over 24 years.

Chris Wicht operated a saloon in Ballarat (shown here) beginning in 1902, when he first arrived, until 1917. This saloon is the site of one of Ballarat's most famous (alleged) incidents. Popular miner Shorty Harris was passed out in Wicht's saloon, and his friends put him in a makeshift coffin and set it on the pool table. They had a eulogy and were carrying the coffin to the graveyard when Shorty woke up. Terrified, Shorty ran out of town.

Ballarat was founded in 1896 as a result of a revival of mining in the Panamint District. The town was the center for miners' activities in the area. In the 1960s, Charles Manson and his family stayed at the Barker ranch south of Ballarat. The movie *Easy Rider* had a scene filmed in Ballarat.

The town of Leadfield, located in Titus Canyon, was founded as a result of a stock swindle by C. C. Julian of Los Angeles. Leadfield had a post office that operated from June 1926 until the end of that year, as well as a population of about 500.

The town of Leadfield prospered in 1926, but as people began to realize there was nothing of substance and that a scam had been perpetrated, the population left in droves. This photograph was taken in 1933, and the toll that was taken in only a few years by the harsh conditions is clearly evident. (Willard.)

This view gives the perspective of riding on the train through Death Valley during the 1920s. The photograph was taken on a Tonopah and Tidewater Railroad engine by the T&T weighmaster W. H. "Brownie" Brown while the engine was passing through a canyon south of Tecopa.

Part of the Tonopah and Tidewater Railroad yard at the Pacific Coast Borax Company town of Death Valley Junction can be seen in this photograph, taken in 1934. The Amargosa Hotel is in the background. In back of the hotel are the Funeral Mountains. The building to the far right has been called the Amargosa Opera House since 1968 and is used for performances by the famous dancer Marta Becket. (Photograph by George J. Capdevielle.)

A Tonopah and Tidewater Railroad worker stands in front of the post office at Silver Lake. Silver Lake was a station on the Tonopah and Tidewater Railroad, which served Death Valley. While not in Death Valley proper, the region can get quite hot, as is evidenced by the handwritten note on this photograph: "122º in shade." The American Railway Express sign dates this picture from 1918 to 1929—the period of operation of American Railway Express, which was formed by a merger of all of the express companies during World War I and was reorganized into Railway Express Agency in 1929. The Silver Lake Post Office operated from 1907 until 1933. Ralph J. "Dad" Fairbanks, who was the last merchant in Greenwater and founded Shoshone, was also the last postmaster at Silver Lake.

# Four

# Death Valley Scotty and Scotty's Castle

Born Walter E. Scott, "Death Valley Scotty" first came to Death Valley in 1885 and worked for the Harmony Borax Works. Leaving the area, he became a cowboy in Buffalo Bill's Wild West Show from 1890 to 1902. After a disagreement with Buffalo Bill, Scotty returned to Death Valley. Using the showmanship skills acquired by observing Buffalo Bill's publicity machine, he began to promote the sale of his "mines" in Death Valley. In 1905, when Scotty chartered a train to break the speed record from Chicago to Los Angeles, he became known nationally. Scotty became a consummate public relations expert who successfully kept his name in the papers for almost 50 years by manipulating the press—including feeding stories and scoops to his good friend Warden Woolard, the city editor of the *Los Angeles Examiner*. Scotty's skill extended to "spinning" negative stories and lawsuits, which followed him all his life. Scotty also loved to be photographed, particularly in the company of movie stars and pretty women. His personal life was not so glamorous, as he was estranged from his wife and son most of his life, sometimes acrimoniously.

One of Scotty's early victims was Albert M. Johnson, a wealthy Chicago insurance man who invested in Scotty's nonexistent mining ventures. Unlike others who were duped by Scotty, Johnson became lifelong friends with Scotty. Johnson provided him with plenty of money and was happy to sit on the sidelines and be amused by Scotty's antics. Johnson enjoyed coming to Death Valley with his wife, Bessie, who wanted a nice place to stay. As a result, Johnson spent about $2 million to build Death Valley Ranch, now known as Scotty's Castle. Begun in 1922 with a smaller structure, building continued until 1931 when the Depression drained Johnson's funds. In 1933, before Death Valley became a national monument, a government survey revealed that Johnson did not own the land on which the castle was being built. A land swap was worked out in 1937, and Johnson obtained ownership; however, he never resumed building and the castle remains unfinished.

Death Valley Scotty (Walter Edward Scott) burst on the national scene in July 1905, when he chartered a train to break the Chicago–Los Angeles speed record. This photograph depicts a young Death Valley Scotty in 1905 or 1906. It was taken in Goldfield by the noted Alaska gold rush photographer Per Larson. Larson made postcards out of the photograph to capitalize on Scotty's growing fame, and they were widely disseminated. The caption "Scotty the Desert Mystery" refers to the mysterious gold mine of fabulous wealth that Scotty claimed to have. Scotty was not shy about publicity and encouraged his mysterious persona.

As soon as Death Valley Scotty broke the Chicago–Los Angeles speed record on the "Scott Special," the Santa Fe Railroad published this 1905 promotional pamphlet. It was one of the first publications to cash in on Death Valley Scotty's rise to national prominence. It gives all of the details of the trip, including photographs of the engines and engineers, timetables, maps, elevations, and a detailed analysis of the trip.

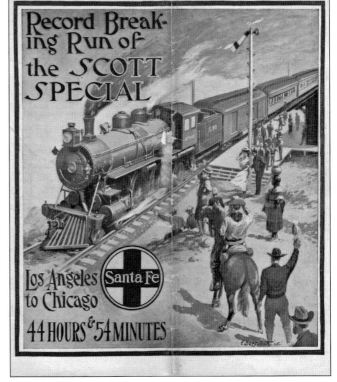

On the back of this card is written: "How would you like to take a chase around the desert in this machine? The fellow in the back seat, right side is the 'Mystery.' Maybe you've seen the lad at the wheel. Started west again yesterday at the same old lace." This card was sent from Goldfield in June 1908. The "mystery" was Death Valley Scotty.

During Scotty's early years of fame, he tried to keep up some appearance of normalcy by having photographs taken with his wife. Here Death Valley Scotty and his wife, Jack, are posing for a picture in front of an office in Rhyolite about 1906. Jack was a passenger on the Scott Special but did not enjoy the resultant publicity. Note her feeble attempt at a smile.

THE STORY OF

"SCOTTY" AND HIS GREAT WESTERN DRAMA

BY CHARLES A. TAYLOR.

Price 25 Cents

WALTER SCOTT
SPHINX OF THE AMERICAN DESERT

KING OF THE DESERT MINE

The first biographies of Scotty appeared shortly after the Scott Special's record-breaking run. The earliest of these were *Mysterious Scott the Monte Christo of Death Valley* by Orin S. Merrill and *The Story of Scotty* by Charles A. Taylor, both written in 1906. *The Story of Scotty* was sold at the play of the same name in which Scotty starred.

Death Valley Scotty is butchering a hog on his Lower Vine Ranch, a few miles from the castle. Although to some people Scotty was a blowhard con man, the reality was much more complex. For 10 years, during the last part of the 19th century, Scotty was a cowboy with Buffalo Bill's Wild West Show before he achieved national fame in Death Valley. (NPS photograph.)

Dressed in his usual outfit, Death Valley Scotty looks the part of the desert prospector he was. This photograph from 1932 of Scotty on a mule leading another mule packed with provisions for a long, solitary excursion into the desert was inscribed and signed by Scotty "to my old friend Willard, City Editor Examiner."

Death Valley Scotty is sitting next to a standing man identified as "Two Gun Charlie," or Charles W. Benton, a sheriff of Goldfield who was said to be "full of guts and thunder and afraid of no man."

Daniel E. Owen, Bill Keys, and Warner Scott (Scotty's brother) were part of an elaborate plan by Death Valley Scotty to scare away investors who demanded to see Scotty's (nonexistent) gold mine, in which they had invested. The plans included a realistic gun battle in which shots were to be fired to dissuade the investors from continuing their quest in the mines. The "Battle of Wingate Pass" was orchestrated by Scotty but did not go as planned. Scotty's brother Warner was severely wounded and nearly died when he was accidentally shot in the groin.

Although Death Valley Scotty lived on the front page for over 50 years, it was not always by his design. The March 3, 1906, *Los Angeles Examiner* gave its entire front page to the Battle of Wingate Pass. Of course the paper did not know it had been Scotty's comrades in arms who ambushed the party and nearly killed Scotty's brother Warner.

Bill Keyes still looks menacing in his later years. Keyes, who was half Cherokee, was an early partner with Death Valley Scotty and was an active participant in the Battle of Wingate Pass. Keyes later was a participant in one of the last gunfights of the West, killing Worth Bagley in 1943, for which he was sent to prison. Keyes case was taken up by attorney Earle Stanley Gardiner, author of the Perry Mason books, and Gardiner was ultimately able to secure a pardon for Keyes. (Murray.)

After Scotty made the "public confession" that his secret gold mine was a big hoax, Julian Gerrard, his first grubstaker, did not believe Scotty's protestations. So, in 1940, Gerrard filed suit in federal court in Los Angeles against Scotty, seeking a share of Scotty's wealth in return for the 1907 grubstake. A smiling Scotty in court shakes hands with Gerrard, while Albert Johnson (the real source of Scotty's wealth) looks on.

Scotty and his dog are going over the plans for the castle with Albert Johnson. The castle was originally conceived as a two-story stucco house, but the plans for the house kept changing until the Spanish-influenced mansion began construction in 1925. Johnson was a Chicago insurance executive who wanted to improve the existing ranch buildings so that when his wife, Bessie, visited Death Valley, she could stay in comfort.

This is a representation of the original design of the castle, which was rendered by C. A. Mac Neilledge of Los Angeles. Scotty with tongue-in-cheek told the tourists that the castle would be surrounded by a moat with man-eating sharks and a drawbridge.

This is thought to be the only known photograph of Death Valley Scotty's wife, Jack, while she was at the castle. It was taken in March 1928 and shows the castle being constructed, as evidenced by the construction equipment and the large excavated hole. Scotty had a tempestuous relationship with Jack, and they lived most of their lives apart.

Bessie Johnson was the wife of Albert Johnson, Death Valley Scotty's benefactor, and is shown here holding a Bible. She was a devout evangelical and would preach Sunday services for the workmen at the castle. Called "Mabel" by Death Valley Scotty, she authored a manuscript titled "Death Valley Scotty by Mabel," which has now been published by the Death Valley Natural History Association. She died in an automobile accident in Death Valley in 1943.

It is estimated that 14,000 concrete fence posts were used to surround Johnson's property in Death Valley. The posts were not only used to establish the boundaries of Johnson's holdings, but also to keep out area ranchers' stock and strengthen his legal claims acquired in connection with water-rights law. Each post is marked with an "S" and a "J" for Scotty and Johnson. The building of the castle can be seen in the background of this 1928 photograph.

During construction of the castle, Albert Johnson hired the Bullfrog Goldfield Railroad to bring building supplies to Bonnie Claire, the station closest to the castle. When the railroad ceased operations in January 1928, Johnson promptly bought 100,000 railroad ties from the abandoned road for use as firewood. Here some of these ties are being hauled to "Tie Canyon" in back of the castle. It was thought that there were enough ties to keep all of the castle's 18 fireplaces going for over 100 years.

Death Valley is known as being one of the hottest places on earth. But, as the picture shows, Death Valley is really a land of extremes. The clock tower at Scotty's Castle was surrounded by snow during a very rare snowstorm that dropped 18 inches during construction of the castle in 1929.

Palm trees are associated with Death Valley and Scotty's Castle, but they are not native. This photograph is marked "Taking in one of the two full grown palms they trucked all the way from L.A. by way of Las Vegas—about 500 miles" and was taken on March 19, 1930, during the construction of Scotty's Castle.

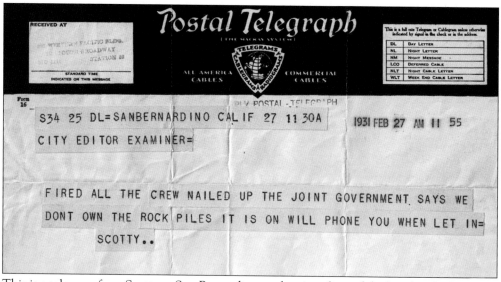

This is a telegram from Scotty at San Bernardino to the city editor of the *Los Angeles Examiner* giving Scotty's version of the controversy with the U.S. government over the dispute as to the exact location of Scotty's Castle. It reads, "Fired all the crew. Nailed up the Joint. Government says we don't own the rock piles it is on. Will phone you when let in. Scotty," and is dated February 27, 1931.

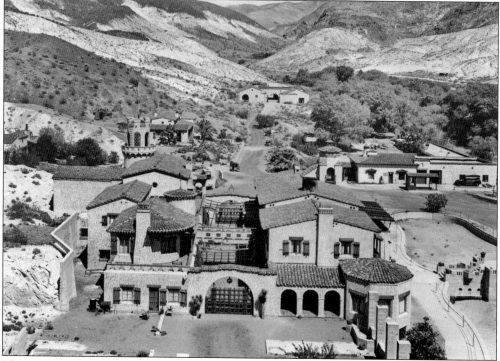

This panoramic photograph of Scotty's Castle shows much of the castle grounds, including a rear view of the main castle building, the unfinished swimming pool, and guest facilities. It was taken from the Chimes Tower. Scotty's apartment (which he did not like to use) is in the bottom left, where his rocking chair also can be seen.

The castel

# HOLLYWOOD PLAZA HOTEL
VINE AT HOLLYWOOD BLVD.
**HOLLYWOOD. CALIF.**

THE DOORWAY OF
HOSPITALITY
AND CALIFORNIA
SUNSHINE

*friend Willard*

*The 20 th Century*
*picture gang sent a*
*man in Here and wanted*
*some kind of a picture*
*of Me I told them*
*if they wanted Help*
*He get a land titel*
*to the castel I wauld*
*sing a gree-ment to*
*that effect I did Not*
*toke a Cent Nor am I*
*to Get a cent*

This is the first page of a letter written by Death Valley Scotty on January 3, 1935, to *Los Angeles Examiner* editor Warden Woolard demonstrating Scotty's efforts to help Johnson with the disputed title issues for the castle. Note Scotty's unusual spelling, which is left uncorrected: "The 20th Century picture gang sent a man in here and wanted some kind of a picture of me. I told them if they would help me get a land title to the castel I would sing a greement to that effect." The letter later goes on to say, "I would like to get titel to castel. I have not seen Johnson nor Mabbel since I saw you. He told me, as I told you, he would deed his half over to me, when he got back from Chicago . . . he has bin gone 11 months. Now that is that." Scotty never did receive "his half." When the title dispute with the federal government was resolved, the title was in Johnson's name, where it remained.

Death Valley Scotty is standing in front of "his castle" with castle managers Henry H. and Gertrude Ringe. The castle opened to tours in 1936, and from the late 1930s until the 1960s, overnight accommodations were available at the castle. Gertrude Ringe served as postmaster of the castle post office for all six years of its operation. This snapshot was taken in 1948.

A highlight for many of those staying at the castle would be a visit with Scotty. A visit provided a popular photo opportunity with Scotty from the balcony in the castle's great hall, such as this one, taken in 1948.

Death Valley Scotty and John Barrymore are seen here in front of Scotty's cabin at Lower Vine Ranch during a weeklong visit by Barrymore in the 1930s. Although Scotty had a bedroom at the castle, he never stayed in it, preferring instead this hideaway cabin a few miles away. It was built by Johnson for Scotty by the same workmen who built the castle.

This candid snapshot, taken in December 1928, shows Death Valley Scotty (in the center wearing a white shirt), Albert Johnson (on the right), and a cowboy named Mills doing ranch work in the horse corral at the Lower Vine Ranch near where Scotty actually lived.

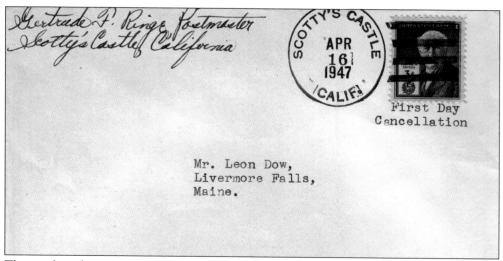

SCOTTY'S CASTLE
APR
16
1947
CALIF.

First Day
Cancellation

Mr. Leon Dow,
Livermore Falls,
Maine.

The number of visitors to Scotty's Castle was constantly increasing, and the post office opened an office there. This envelope was mailed in 1947 on the first day that the post office at Scotty's Castle was open and was sent by Gertrude F. Ringe, the postmaster. The post office ceased operations on May 15, 1953.

Death Valley Scotty and partner Albert M. Johnson peer into Ubehebe Crater, located not too far from Scotty's Castle. A shrewd businessman, Johnson tried to obtain title to as much of the surrounding acreage to his castle as he could. In addition to outright purchase, Johnson and his team of lawyers would acquire land titles through possession of water rights and mining rights. Ultimately, Johnson was very successful, owning over 1.5 million acres.

In this atypical portrait, Death Valley Scotty is holding a rifle in front of an ornately detailed metal door to "his" castle. Note the grim no-nonsense expression on his face, in sharp contrast with his public persona of good old boy storyteller.

| License Issued | May 6 1942 | APPLICATION FOR OPERATOR'S LICENSE | | No. R 415729 Restrictions | | |
|---|---|---|---|---|---|---|
| License Expires | May 6 1946 | | | | | |
| Full Name | | WALTER SCOTT (DEATH VALLEY | | | | |
| Street No. | | SCOTTYS CASTLE "SCOTTY) | | | | |
| City | | DEATHVALLEY VIA GOLDFIELD NEVADA | | | | SUPPLEMENTARY ADDRESS |

| SEX (M.F) | HEIGHT | DATE OF BIRTH | | | |
|---|---|---|---|---|---|
| M | 5/10 | SEPT 20 1873 | | | |
| WEIGHT | COLOR EYES | COLOR HAIR | RACE | | |
| 200 | BLUE | GRAY | WHITE | | RIGHT THUMB PRINT |
| PREVIOUS LICENSE NUMBER | | YEAR ISSUED | MARRIED? | AGE | |
| G338925 | | 1938 | YES | 69 | |

CHANGE OF ADDRESS MUST BE REPORTED TO DEPARTMENT WITHIN 10 DAYS. VEHICLE CODE. SEC. 331

I HEREBY CERTIFY, THAT THE PERSON DESCRIBED HEREON HAS BEEN GRANTED THE PRIVILEGE OF OPERATING MOTOR VEHICLES, SUBJECT TO ANY RESTRICTIONS CONTAINED HEREON.

SIGNATURE OF LICENSEE          DIVISION OF DRIVERS LICENSES
                              Paul Mason  Chief of Division

| Date MAY - 6 1942 | | | Office | Death Valley | | | |
|---|---|---|---|---|---|---|---|
| Without Glasses | B20 /30 | R20 /30 | L20 /30 | Traffic Signs | P | F | Oral | P | F |
| With Glasses | B20/ | R20/ | L20/ | Hearing | P | F | Written | P X F |
| Restrictions | | | | Driving | | | P X F |

APP. No 794802

Seen here is Death Valley Scotty's 1942 California driver's license, signed by Scotty. Note that his address is Scotty's Castle, Death Valley via Goldfield Nevada and that his name, "Death Valley Scotty," is listed parenthetically after his given name, Walter Scott. Scotty was 5 feet, 10 inches tall, weighed a sturdy 200 pounds, and had blue eyes.

Death Valley Scotty did not spend all of his time in the desert. In this 1931 photograph, Scotty is shown attending a Warner Brothers Hollywood movie premiere. He is accompanied by Mrs. Robert W. Walsh (left) and Lillian Pollard. Scotty claimed Joseph Pollard, the father of these two sisters, was his old-time friend.

This is another of the many photographs of Scotty posing with a movie star, although this time Albert Johnson is in the photograph as well (far left). Scotty is in the middle, and William S. Hart is on the far right, surrounded by nurses. The picture was taken in an unidentified location.

These contrasting photographs depict the "real" Death Valley Scotty (left) and the version portrayed by Jack Lomas (right). Lomas played Scotty in the 1955 episode of the *Death Valley Days* television show titled "Death Valley Scotty," which recreated Scotty's record-breaking train run on the Scott Special.

Never shy about self-promotion, Death Valley Scotty embarked on a personal publicity campaign in the 1930s in which he would stage photo opportunities with the motion picture stars of the day. Here Scotty is pretending to give pointers to actors Bette Davis and Leslie Howard at the Warner Brothers Studio in Burbank, California. (Photograph by Ed Stine.)

Death Valley Scotty and T. R. Goodwin, superintendent of Death Valley National Monument, are enjoying a chat at the castle. Goodwin was instrumental in taking up the cause of the native Timbisha to prevent their removal from the monument during the 1930s, when conventional thought was that the lifestyle of the Timbisha was exhausting the sparse wildlife. (Photograph by Tom G. Murray.)

Harry Oliver is shown sleeping in Death Valley Scotty's bed at Scotty's Castle. Harry Oliver became the editor of the *Desert Rat Scrapbook* after having been a set designer in Hollywood and receiving two Academy Award nominations during the late 1920s. The photograph of Buffalo Bill relates to Scotty's early days when he was a cowboy in Buffalo Bill's Wild West Show. (Photography by Tom G. Murray.)

Mr. and Mrs. Walter P. Scott and their daughter are standing in front of the door leading to the great hall, where Scotty usually entertained his guests. Walter was Scotty's only child. Scotty did not have very much to do with his wife and son and lived alone. (Photograph by Tom G. Murray.)

This is Slim's Bar and Café at Scotty's Junction, near where Scotty died while being rushed to the hospital in 1954. His body was brought into the café and laid on the floor until the undertaker from Goldfield arrived. The café has since burned to the ground.

"Death Valley Scotty lies in his coffin in front of the huge fireplace in the great hall of the castle. The chairs where Johnson and Scotty sat entertaining their guests were roped off. Only the castle's help and a few friends attended the funeral. It was a quick service because it was feared that the park rangers would not be able to handle the thousands of cars that would jam the narrow roads. Scotty died on January 9, 1954, and is buried with his dog on a hill, a short walk from the back of the castle.

# Five

# TOURISM

Today tourism has replaced mining as the main economic activity in Death Valley. Camping was the earliest and only form of overnight accommodation initially available in Death Valley. Though many towns did spring up in Death Valley, none have survived that can accommodate tourists (nearby Beatty, Nevada, is an exception). Seeing a niche that could be filled, former Rhyolite miner and Catalina Tour operator H. W. "Bob" Eichbaum and his wife, Helene, constructed a toll road from Darwin into Death Valley and built the resort now known as Stovepipe Wells, which opened in November 1926

At the same time the Eichbaums were constructing their toll road and hotel, the upscale Furnace Creek Inn was being constructed by the Pacific Coast Borax Company. It opened early in 1927. In addition, the Pacific Coast Borax Company dormitories at Death Valley Junction were converted into the Death Valley Inn, and the dormitories at Ryan were converted to the Desert View Inn. Even Scotty's Castle offered tourist lodging for a time. The resort at Panamint Springs was built by William and Agnes Cody Reid in 1937 and afforded the tourist the choice of a campground or basic motel facilities, as well as a gas station.

Tourists come to see the magnificent scenery, and many come to Death Valley just to experience its heat. Badwater, at 282 feet below sea level, is the lowest point in North America. It also happens to be the hottest place in the western hemisphere, with a recorded temperature of 134 degrees. Ground temperatures at Furnace Creek can reach over 200 degrees. Many films have been shot on location in Death Valley to take advantage of its stark and beautiful scenery. Death Valley became a national monument in 1933 and a national park in 1994.

In 1949, as a part of California's centennial, the 100-year anniversary of the ordeal of the original Death Valley gold-seeking party was commemorated by a large-scale reenactment and "encampment." It was so popular that the tradition continues as an annual celebration to this day and is held every November.

Mushroom Rock became a tourist destination and photo opportunity when a road was constructed to it about 1930. A name change was proposed—the Devil's Throne—but was not adopted. One of the first tourists using this road posed to have his picture taken next to his car at Mushroom Rock in 1930.

The Caulfield family is seen posing in front of the Devil's Golf Course sign. The Devil's Golf Course is an evaporated lake bed with crystal salt deposits that formed in many unusual shapes. In 1927, shortly after this photograph was taken, the first 3 holes of the Furnace Creek Golf Course were built—subsequently enlarged to 9 holes in 1931 and 18 holes in 1968.

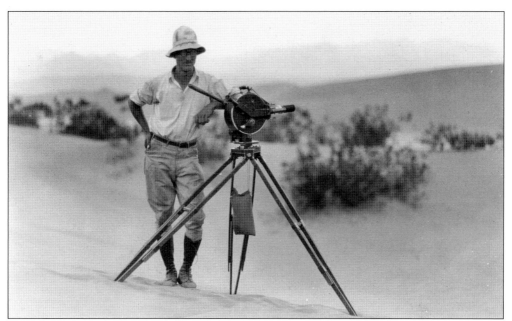

William A. Sickner was a director of photography on over 50 Hollywood movies from 1935 to 1962. In the 1920s, he was an Akeley Camera operator and is shown here in Death Valley in 1926, possibly working on the film *The Wagon Show*, which was released in early 1928.

This is the cast and crew on location at Sheep Mountain in Death Valley during the filming of the motion picture *Greed* during the summer of 1923. Based on Frank Norris's novel *McTeague*, *Greed* was the first feature film shot entirely on location, and because it was filmed during the height of the summer's heat, many suffered from heat prostration and illness.

Although many films were shot in Death Valley, *Panamint's Bad Man*, starring Smith Ballew, Stanley Fields, Noah Beery, and Evelyn Daw, was not one of them. The subject matter and the plot were set in Death Valley, but it was filmed elsewhere—as was also the case with the film *The Parson from Panamint*.

Actor Gilbert Gowland can be seen boarding a Death Valley Railroad train car during the filming of Erich von Stroheim's motion picture *Greed* in 1923. The Death Valley Railroad ran from Death Valley Junction to Ryan. Built originally to haul Ryan's ore to market, it subsequently served tourists from 1927 to 1930, when both towns converted their housing to accommodate paying guests.

A Utah Parks Company touring car sits in front of sand dunes in Death Valley near Stovepipe Wells. The card was mailed from Ryan on March 19, 1928, and written at Furnace Creek. "Have been taking an auto trip through Death Valley," the card reads. Auto or stage tours continued in Death Valley until 1930, when the automobile roads had improved enough to entice tourists to travel on their own. (Willard.)

After World War II, the Death Valley region became a favorite spot for "rock hounding" and exploring, as witnessed by the hundreds of articles in *Desert Magazine* during the 1940s, 1950s, and 1960s. Rock hounding was a popular hobby for many who collect rock and mineral specimens in the desert. Shown here is a College of the Pacific field trip made to the desert, which included a trip to Death Valley.

Pictured is Bob Eichbaum (left) camping in Death Valley with Bill Ball in 1906. At the time this photograph was taken, Eichbaum and Ball were in the process of building the electric plant in Rhyolite. Note the log cabin syrup tin that can be seen on the ground.

Bob Eichbaum, who had been a part of Rhyolite's boom, left Death Valley to run a sightseeing business on Catalina Island. He wanted to capitalize on his knowledge of the tourist trade by building a hotel in Death Valley. He realized that in addition to a hotel there would have to be a road so tourists could get to it. He proceeded to build a toll road from Darwin into Death Valley and the hotel at Stovepipe Wells.

Bob and Helene Eichbaum are seen here on the porch of the Dow Hotel in Lone Pine in 1923. G. W. Dow was instrumental in providing assistance to the Eichbaums during the construction of the Eichbaums' toll road into Death Valley. Helene Eichbaum was acknowledged to be the first nonnative woman to make permanent residence in Death Valley.

This photograph shows the early camp of Bob and Helene Eichbaum in Death Valley. The construction equipment that was being used to build the toll road from Darwin to Death Valley got stuck in the sandy terrain here so they built the Stove Pipe Wells Hotel on this site. Known as Bungalow City, it was Death Valley's first tourist resort.

This is an early view of Stove Pipe Wells when it was still referred to as Bungalow or Bungalette City. Bob Eichbaum can be seen standing at the far right next to the two cars at the terminus of the road. Eichbaums' toll road is credited for having changed the Death Valley region's economic base from mining to tourism.

Seen here is an entrance sign for the tollgate at the start of the Death Valley Toll Road in Darwin Wash. The small sign at the right gives the toll rates at $2 per car and 50¢ per person and states that the distance to Stove Pipe Wells is 31 miles.

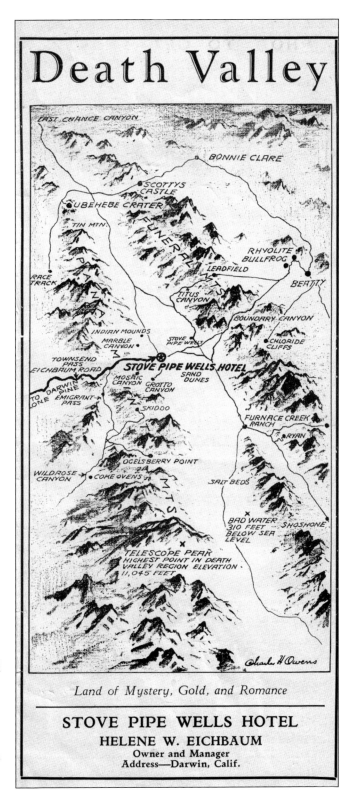

# Death Valley

EAST CHANCE CANYON
BONNIE CLARE
SCOTTYS CASTLE
UBEHEBE CRATER
TIN MTN.
FUNERAL
RHYOLITE
BULLFROG
LEADFIELD
RACE TRACK
BEATTY
TITUS CANYON
BOUNDARY CANYON
INDIAN MOUNDS
MARBLE CANYON
STOVE PIPE WELLS
CHLORIDE CLIFFS
TOWNSEND PASS
EICHBAUM ROAD
STOVE PIPE WELLS HOTEL
MOSAIC CANYON
SAND DUNES
GROTTO CANYON
TO DARWIN
LONE EMIGRANT PASS
SKIDOO
FURNACE CREEK RANCH
RYAN
OGELSBERRY POINT
WILDROSE CANYON
COKE OVENS
SALT BEDS
MTS
BAD WATER 310 FEET BELOW SEA LEVEL
SHOSHONE
TELESCOPE PEAK HIGHEST POINT IN DEATH VALLEY REGION ELEVATION 11,045 FEET

*Charles H Owens*

Land of Mystery, Gold, and Romance

## STOVE PIPE WELLS HOTEL
### HELENE W. EICHBAUM
Owner and Manager
Address—Darwin, Calif.

This map was a part of a Stove Pipe Wells Hotel advertising brochure. It depicts the principal points of interest in Death Valley for tourists about 1932. Many of these remain popular places to visit today. The road through Death Valley ran from Olancha to Darwin to the Stove Pipe Wells Hotel via the Eichbaum Road. Note that owner Helene Eichbaum's address is given in Darwin because that was the nearest post office.

John Weigand was a caretaker at Stove Pipe Wells in the early days of the resort. Tall tales were constantly told to visitors by the early Death Valley workers and inhabitants. A popular tale about Weigand was that he was able to make $20 bills "grow" on sagebrush.

This small Stove Pipe Wells Hotel advertising insert lists all the tourist attractions to visit in Death Valley. Tourists today still visit most of them, although some now require a four-wheel-drive or high-clearance vehicle. The advertisement dates from 1932.

Tourist cabins were built in Darwin to take advantage of the tourist boom to Death Valley created by the Eichbaums' toll road, which started just outside of Darwin and effectively made Darwin the western gateway to Death Valley. Darwin held this position until the present State Route 190, which bypasses Darwin, was built.

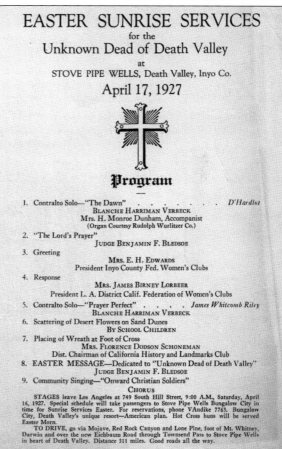

EASTER SUNRISE SERVICES
for the
Unknown Dead of Death Valley
at
STOVE PIPE WELLS, Death Valley, Inyo Co.

April 17, 1927

### Program

1. Contralto Solo—"The Dawn" . . . . . . . . . . D'Hardlot
   BLANCHE HARRIMAN VERBECK
   Mrs. H. Monroe Dunham, Accompanist
   (Organ Courtesy Rudolph Wurlitzer Co.)
2. "The Lord's Prayer"
   JUDGE BENJAMIN F. BLEDSOE
3. Greeting
   MRS. E. H. EDWARDS
   President Inyo County Fed. Women's Clubs
4. Response
   MRS. JAMES BIRNEY LORBEER
   President L. A. District Calif. Federation of Women's Clubs
5. Contralto Solo—"Prayer Perfect" . . . . . James Whitcomb Riley
   BLANCHE HARRIMAN VERBECK
6. Scattering of Desert Flowers on Sand Dunes
   BY SCHOOL CHILDREN
7. Placing of Wreath at Foot of Cross
   MRS. FLORENCE DODSON SCHONEMAN
   Dist. Chairman of California History and Landmarks Club
8. EASTER MESSAGE—Dedicated to "Unknown Dead of Death Valley"
   JUDGE BENJAMIN F. BLEDSOE
9. Community Singing—"Onward Christian Soldiers"
   CHORUS

STAGES leave Los Angeles at 749 South Hill Street, 9:00 A.M., Saturday, April 16, 1927. Special schedule will take passengers to Stove Pipe Wells Bungalow City in time for Sunrise Services Easter. For reservations, phone VAndike 7763. Bungalow City, Death Valley's unique resort—American plan. Hot Cross buns will be served Easter Morn.

TO DRIVE, go via Mojave, Red Rock Canyon and Lone Pine, foot of Mt. Whitney, Darwin and over the new Eichbaum Road through Townsend Pass to Stove Pipe Wells in heart of Death Valley. Distance 311 miles. Good roads all the way.

This program is for the Easter sunrise services for the unknown dead of Death Valley held at Stove Pipe Wells, April 17, 1927. The services were arranged by the Eichbaums to promote their new resort, then known as Bungalow City. The directions include going to Darwin and then "over the new Eichbaum Road."

This is an early view of the Furnace Creek Inn, taken during construction. The idea for building the Furnace Creek Inn originally was conceived by railroad and borax man Frank Jenifer. The idea was spurred into reality when the Pacific Coast Borax Company felt that Bob Eichbaum's toll road and hotel would result in a monopoly for the emerging tourist trade. (Willard.)

Guests are seen bathing in the Furnace Creek Inn swimming pool in this photograph, taken in the early 1930s, a few years after the Furnace Creek Inn opened. The Furnace Creek Inn featured first-class accommodations to compete with the more spartan rooms offered by Bob Eichbaum and his Stove Pipe Wells Hotel.

This is one of the first brochures promoting the Furnace Creek Inn, *c.* 1927–1928. The inn billed itself as "possibly the most uniquely situated hotel in the world," and boasted that it "is modern and first-class in every respect." It opened in 1927 and was built to draw tourists from the Eichbaums' toll road and hotel.

The Furnace Creek Inn opened in 1927, three months after the completion of Bob Eichbaum's toll road and his hotel, Bungalow City. The Furnace Creek Inn, however, featured more luxurious accommodations and amenities. This snapshot photograph of the inn was taken on a trip through Death Valley in 1930.

The Furnace Creek Inn is the site for a reenactment of the 20-mule team and borax wagons, favorites of Death Valley tourists for several generations. The 20-mule team, a recognizable image for Death Valley, was continually used in advertising and promotions for over a century. (Photograph by Harry Gower.)

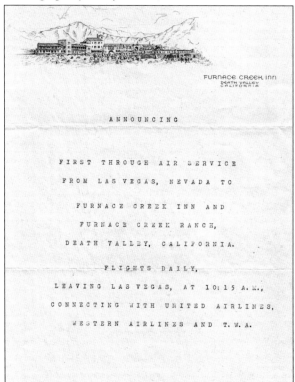

Seen here is a November 1953 announcement for the commencement of Bonanza Air Lines' first through-air services between the Furnace Creek Inn at Death Valley and Las Vegas. It was sent on the first flight to the wife of Horace Albright, the 1933 director of the National Park Service who was instrumental in having Death Valley named a national monument.

Maj. Julian Boyd took over as mining superintendent of Borax Consolidator's operations at Ryan in 1920. When the company closed down the mines in 1927, the miners' dormitories at Ryan were turned into the Death Valley View Hotel, and Boyd served as its manager—and as postmaster for the town. The hotel and post office both ceased operations in 1930.

The Death Valley Hotel Company operated a hotel in Ryan. Owned by the Pacific Coast Borax Company, the hotel rooms were converted miners' dormitories from when Ryan was the company town. This one-page advertisement is contained in one of the first brochures promoting the first-class tourist facilities at the Furnace Creek Inn, around 1927. Note that the accommodations in Ryan were certainly not first-class.

3. A View of the Cottages at Ryan

4. A Section of the Community Dining Room

1. The Community of Ryan from Below in the Valley

2. The Entrance to One of the Borax Mines

6. The Gasoline Motor Coach of the Death Valley Railroad Which Makes the Trip Between Ryan and Death Valley Junction

5. A Living Room in One of the Cottages at Ryan

## RYAN, CALIFORNIA

MAJOR J. BOYD, *Manager*

At Ryan one finds full accommodations the year round for any length of stay. Completely furnished cottages are available with hot and cold water, electric lights, fuel, bed linen and table silver all provided. These cottages rent for $120 by the month; by the day, the charge is $2.50 for a single guest and $4.00 for the double accommodations. Excellent meals are served in the community dining room at $1.00 each.

There is a general store and market where fresh fruits, vegetables and meats are sold with a complete line of other necessities. Moving pictures are exhibited once a week and a community dance adds weekly to the numerous sources of amusement. An excellent tennis court is at the disposal of guests.

There is a hospital in Ryan and a physician is on call at Death Valley Junction.

Ryan has an altitude of 3,007 feet above sea level, a feature which insures moderate daytime temperatures and cool evenings the year round.

The Amargosa Hotel at Death Valley Junction originally served as dormitories for the Pacific Coast Borax Company. It was also known as the Death Valley Inn. The building complex has been the home of the Amargosa Opera House since 1967 and is operated with performances by famed dancer Marta Beckett. (Willard.)

This tow truck bears markings as being from the Death Valley Junction Garage. The photograph, taken at Death Valley Junction, looks as though William H. "Brownie" Brown (far left) and friends are burying or digging up a wooden coffin in the local cemetery. The back of the photograph cryptically identifies it as being from Willard E. Schmidt, "chief Internal Security Manzanar, Calif." Manzanar was the relocation center used for incarcerating Japanese Americans during World War II.

"Death Valley Wonder" is the title of this novelty photograph, which was sold to early Death Valley tourists. This photograph is dated February 14, 1908, with a note on the back that reads, "Hello Conda: Come out and I will give you a ride on one of my animals on opposite side."

This staged photograph was taken in front of a sign proclaiming "Death Valley Inn," probably in a photographer's studio, and is dated 1913. The fascination with Death Valley predated the tourist industry. Although there ultimately were two different Death Valley Inns, this location is in a photographer's studio, probably in Canada. A number of photographs have been seen with this same setting but showing different people. In this and all of the other similar photographs, the subjects are wearing angora chaps, which never would have been worn in the 120-degree temperatures of Death Valley.

A visitor driving to a national park or monument in the 1930s would have paid an entrance fee and received a decal to stick on their windshield. Each park featured a different design: a bison for Yellowstone, a mountain lion for Yosemite, and a covered wagon for Death Valley National Monument. The back of the sticker, the side facing the driver, has the words "safety first" and the name of the park.

What at first looks like another of Death Valley's victims on closer examination reveals a posed photograph taken by a tourist on a 1920s visit to Death Valley. The name Death Valley has captured the imagination of tourists for over a century.

Fr. John J. Crowley was born in 1891 and died in a car accident in 1940. He was known as the "Desert Padre" and ministered to Catholics in the Owens Valley, Death Valley, and Randsburg. Father Crowley Point is located just within the boundary of Death Valley National Park. The memorial at the point was paid for by Helen Gunn Edwards, the words were written by Ralph Merritt, and the plaque was sculpted by Cyria Henderson. Crowley Lake is also named for him.

## BREAKFAST SUGGESTIONS

| | | |
|---|---|---|
| Pineapple Juice | | 10c |
| Orange Juice ... 10c | Grapefruit Juice | 10c |
| Tomato Juice | | 10c |
| Dish of Fruit | | 10c |
| Corn Flakes or Grapenuts | | 15c |
| Cooked Cereal | | 15c |

**1** Stack of Hotcakes and Coffee .... 30c  **2** Stack of Hotcakes with Ham, Bacon or Sausage ...... 50c

**3** 2 Eggs (any style) with Ham, Bacon or Sausage, Toast .. 65c  **4** French Toast, Marmalade, Bacon .. 50c

**5** Minced Ham Omlette ........ 50c  **6** Waffle and Coffee ——35c——

**7** Toast and Coffee ——30c——

| | | | |
|---|---|---|---|
| Coffee | 10c | Milk | 10c |
| Tea | 10c | Chocolate | 15c |

### Desserts

| | |
|---|---|
| Pie, per cut | 15c |
| Pie, A la Mode | 25c |
| Cake, per cut | 15c |
| Ice Cream | 15c |
| Chocolate Sundae | 20c |
| Fresh Strawberry Sundae | 25c |
| Milk Shake | 20c |

#### Sandwiches

| | |
|---|---|
| Ham (home baked) | 25c |
| Tuna | 25c |
| Swiss Cheese | 20c |
| American Cheese | 20c |
| Peanut Butter | 20c |
| Ham and Egg | 30c |
| Deviled Egg | 25c |
| Ham and Cheese | 30c |
| Hamburger | 25c |
| Panamint Special (Tuna and Melted Cheese) | 30c |
| Prospector's Delight (Corned Beef) | 25c |

——Including Potato Chips and Pickle——

## DINNER MENU

| | |
|---|---|
| T-Bone Steak | $1.15 |
| Rib Steak | 1.00 |
| Lamb Chops | .85 |
| Pork Chops | .85 |
| ✓ Chicken Fried Steak | .85 |
| Baked Ham | .85 |
| Hamburger Steak | .75 |
| Roast Beef, Pork or Lamb | .75 |
| Minced Ham Omelette | .75 |

Dinner includes Soup or Tomato
Juice, Salad, Vegetables,
Dessert and Drink

☆

### Beverages

| | |
|---|---|
| Coffee | 10c |
| Tea | 10c |
| Milk | 10c |
| Hot Chocolate | 15c |
| Budweiser Beer | 25c |
| Rainer Ale | 25c |
| Acme Beer | 20c |
| Ginger Ale | 15c |
| Coco Cola, etc. | 10c |

## PANAMINT SPRINGS CAFE

This menu is for the café at the Panamint Springs Resort while it was still being operated by its original builder/owners Bill Reid and Agnes Cody Reid. Bessie Ray wrote the following on the front of this menu: "Had a lovely dinner here Saturday evening February 24, 1940."

Cy Babcock's store at Wildrose Station is seen here still under construction in 1933. Upon completion it would boast tourist cabins, a store, eating facilities, and a gas station. Earlier, Wildrose Station served as a stage station on the Ballarat-Skidoo road and was a stop for prospectors since the 1870s.

This photograph, taken in 1934, shows the interior of the Wildrose Station Store. From left to right are Ambrose Aguereberry, an unidentified National Park Service worker, John Thorndike, C. O. Mittendorf, and Tom Divine. At the time this photograph was taken, Cy Babcock was the owner and operator of Wildrose.

After Cy Babcock, Wildrose Station was owned by the Sample family, who operated it as a store, motel, service station, and a restaurant. There have been no commercial enterprises at Wildrose since 1972, when the National Park Service deemed it unsafe for tourism. Most of the structures were removed.

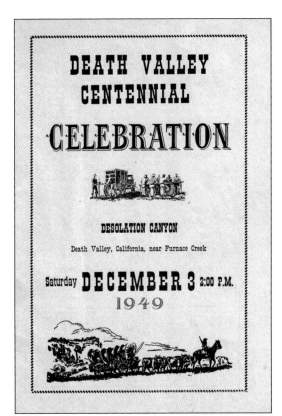

The Death Valley Centennial Celebration was held in December 1949. It was a part of the California Centennial celebrations held during that year, and due to its popularity, became the first of an annual tradition, the Death Valley '49ers Encampment.

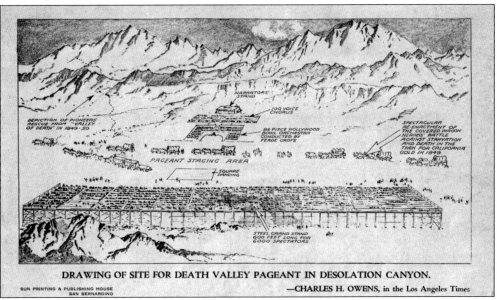

DRAWING OF SITE FOR DEATH VALLEY PAGEANT IN DESOLATION CANYON.

—CHARLES H. OWENS, in the Los Angeles Times

This map was on the back page of the program for the Death Valley Centennial Celebration, which was held in December 1949. It depicts the grounds for the Death Valley Pageant, held in connection with the celebration. Note the grand scope of the proceedings: a wagon train crossing the valley, an 86-piece Hollywood Bowl orchestra, pioneers rescue, etc. The event was attended by about 65,000 people.

G. Henry Stetson (of the famous hat family) was the official starter for the Burro Flapjack Sweepstakes at Stove Pipe Wells during the Death Valley '49ers Encampment in November 1962. Pictured with Stetson is "Death Valley Smiley." The encampment is an annual event, held every November, and is sponsored by the Death Valley '49ers organization. It was first held in 1949, the 100-year anniversary of the first gold seekers to cross Death Valley. (Photograph by Tom G. Murray.)

"Badwater Bill" (Arnold Theodore Fryck) and Princess Whitefeather are participating in the festivities at Stove Pipe Wells during the 15th Death Valley '49ers Encampment. They are dressed in costume and standing next to a team of oxen that was used during the celebration. They both were present when the bronze monument marker at Ballarat was dedicated at that encampment. (Photograph by Tom G. Murray.)

Dr. Edmund C. Jaeger, noted desert naturalist and author of several books on Death Valley, is sitting on the lawn at the Furnace Creek Visitor Center. A species of desert yucca, the *Yucca brevifolia jaegeriana* was named for Jaeger, who did the first comprehensive study of the species in 1935. (Photograph by Tom G. Murray.)

Old-timers are seen here posing at Furnace Creek Ranch Golf Course in November 1965. From left to right are Charles Scholl, former superintendent of the Pacific Coast Borax Company; Randall Henderson, former owner and publisher of *Desert Magazine*; Horace Albright, who cofounded the National Park Service in 1916 and helped make Death Valley a national monument; Hazel Henderson, who served as president of the Death Valley '49ers in 1966; and Harry Gower, former geologist of the Pacific Coast Borax Company and postmaster of Death Valley. (Photograph by Tom G. Murray.)

The skull logo was used in many of the promotions for Death Valley to encourage the exotic location for tourism. This compares with the 20-mule team logo, which was used 40 years earlier as a trademark by the Pacific Coast Borax Company to promote its borax-based products.

The famous sand dunes of Death Valley seem virtually unchanged from when the first pioneers ventured into the valley. They are constantly shifting and are continually on the move in the valley (actually Death Valley is a basin). The sand dunes are located near Stove Pipe Wells Village and range in height from 50 to 400 feet. They remain a popular tourist destination. While this photograph appears to have been taken yesterday, it was taken in 1923.

# BIBLIOGRAPHY

Many books have been published on Death Valley and its surrounding areas. The following small selection covers their respective topics in depth and have extensive related bibliographies for further reading.

Green, Linda W. and Latschar, John A. *Historic Resource Study: A History of Mining in Death Valley National Monument*. Denver: National Park Service, 1981.

Johnston, Hank. *Death Valley Scotty "The Fastest Con in the West."* Corona del Mar: Trans-Anglo Books, 1974.

Lingenfelter, Richard. E. *Death Valley & The Amargosa*. Berkeley: University of California Press, 1986.

Myrick, David F. *Railroads of Nevada and Eastern California*. Berkeley: Howell-North Books, 1963.

Palazzo, Robert P. *Darwin, California*. Lake Grove: Western Places, 1996.

Palazzo, Robert P. Post *Offices and Postmasters of Inyo County, California 1866-1966*. Fernley: Doug MacDonald, 2005.

Patera, Alan H., and David A. Wright. *Skido!* Lake Grove: Western Places, 1999.

Schafer, Leo. *Greenwater, California Death Valley Ghost Town*. Las Vegas: Book Connection, LLC, 2003.

# DISCOVER THOUSANDS OF LOCAL HISTORY BOOKS
## FEATURING MILLIONS OF VINTAGE IMAGES

Arcadia Publishing, the leading local history publisher in the United States, is committed to making history accessible and meaningful through publishing books that celebrate and preserve the heritage of America's people and places.

Find more books like this at
**www.arcadiapublishing.com**

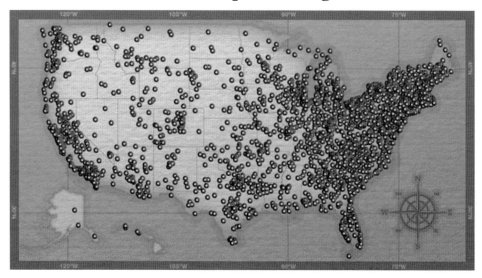

Search for your hometown history, your old stomping grounds, and even your favorite sports team.

Consistent with our mission to preserve history on a local level, this book was printed in South Carolina on American-made paper and manufactured entirely in the United States. Products carrying the accredited Forest Stewardship Council (FSC) label are printed on 100 percent FSC-certified paper.